REDISCOVERING THE MISSING JEWEL

A Study in Worship through the Centuries

REDISCOVERING THE MISSING JEWEL
A Study in Worship through the Centuries

Robert E. Webber

The Alleluia! Series of the Institute for Worship Studies

Hendrickson Publishers, Inc.
P. O. Box 3473
Peabody, Massachusetts 01961-3473

REDISCOVERING THE MISSING JEWEL:
A Study in Worship through the Centuries
by Robert E. Webber

ISBN 1-56563-257-5

Second printing, March 2001

Printed in the United States of America

CONTENTS

WELCOME TO THE
ALLELUIA! SERIES

This Bible study series has been designed by the Institute for Worship Studies primarily for laypersons in the church.

We are living in a time when worship has become a distinct priority for the church. For years, the church has emphasized evangelism, teaching, fellowship, missions, and service to society to the neglect of the very source of its power—worship. But in recent years we have witnessed a Spirit-led renewal in the study and practice of worship.

Because worship has been neglected for so many years, there is precious little information and teaching on the subject in our seminaries, Bible schools, and local churches.

The mission of the Institute for Worship Studies is to make the study of worship available to everyone in the church—academician, pastor, worship leader, music minister, and layperson.

Laypersons will find the seven courses of the Alleluia! Series to be inspiring, informative, and life changing. Each course of study is rooted in biblical teaching, draws from the rich historical treasures of the church, and is highly practical and accessible.

The Institute for Worship Studies presents this course, *Rediscovering the Missing Jewel: A Study of Worship through the Centuries*, as a service to the local church and to its ministry of worship to God. May this study warm your heart, inform your mind, and kindle your spirit. May it inspire and set on fire the worship of the local church. And may this study minister to the church and to the One, Holy, Triune God in whose name it is offered.

THE SEVEN COURSES IN THE ALLELUIA! WORSHIP SERIES

Learning to Worship with All Your Heart: A Study in the Biblical Foundations of Christian Worship

You are led into the rich teachings of worship in both the Old and the New Testaments. Learn the vocabulary of worship, be introduced to theological themes, and study various descriptions of worship. Each lesson inspires you to worship at a deeper level—from the inside out.

Rediscovering the Missing Jewel: A Study in Worship through the Centuries
This stretching course introduces you to the actual worship styles of Christians in other centuries and geographical locations. Study the history of the early, medieval, Reformation, modern, and contemporary periods of worship. Learn from them how your worship today may be enriched, inspired, and renewed. Each lesson introduces you to rich treasures of worship adaptable for contemporary use.

Renew Your Worship: A Study in the Blending of Traditional and Contemporary Worship
This inspiring course leads you into a deeper understanding and experience of your Sunday worship. How does worship bring the congregation into the presence of God, mold the people by the Word, and feed the believers spiritually? The answer to these and other questions will bring a new spiritual depth to your experience of worship.

Enter His Courts with Praise: A Study of the Role of Music and the Arts in Worship
This course introduces you to the powerful way the arts can communicate the mystery of God at work in worship. Music, visual arts, drama, dance, and mime are seen as means through which the gospel challenges the congregation and changes lives.

Rediscovering the Christian Feasts: A Study in the Services of the Christian Year
This stimulating and stretching course helps you experience the traditional church calendar with new eyes. It challenges the secular concept of time and shows how the practice of the Christian year offers an alternative to secularism and shapes the Christian's day-to-day experience of time, using the gospel as its grid.

Encountering the Healing Power of God: A Study in the Sacred Actions of Worship
This course makes a powerful plea for the recovery of those sacred actions that shape the spiritual life. Baptism, Communion, anointing with oil, and other sacred actions are all interpreted with reflection on the death and resurrection of Jesus. These actions shape the believer's spiritual experience into a continual pattern of death to sin and rising to life in the Spirit.

Empowered by the Holy Spirit: A Study in the Ministries of Worship
This course will challenge you to see the relationship between worship and life in the secular world. It empowers the believer in evangelism, spiritual formation, social action, care ministries, and other acts of love and charity.

Take all seven courses and earn a Certificate of Worship Studies (CWS). For more information, call the Institute for Worship Studies at (630) 510-8905.

INTRODUCTION

Rediscovering the Missing Jewel: A Study in Worship through the Centuries may be used for personal study or a small-group course of study and spiritual formation. It is designed around thirteen easy-to-understand sessions. Each session has a two-part study guide. The first part is an individual study that each person completes privately. The second part is a one-hour interaction and application session that group members complete together (during the week or in an adult Sunday school setting). The first part helps you recall and reflect on what you've read, while the small-group study applies the material to each member's personal life and experience of public worship.

Rediscovering the Missing Jewel is designed for use by one or more people. When the course is used in a group setting, the person who is designated as the leader simply needs to lead the group through the lesson step by step. It is always best to choose a leader before you begin.

Here are some suggestions for making your group discussions lively and insightful.

SUGGESTIONS FOR THE STUDENT

A few simple guidelines will help you use the study guide most effectively. They can be summarized under three headings: Prepare, Participate, and Apply.

Prepare

1. Answer each question in the study guide, "Part I: Personal Study," thoughtfully and critically.

2. Do all your work prayerfully. Prayer itself is worship. As you increase your knowledge of worship, do so in a spirit of prayerful openness before God.

Participate

1. Don't be afraid to ask questions. Your questions may give voice to the other members in the group. Your courage in speaking out will give others permission to talk and may encourage more stimulating discussion.

2. Don't hesitate to share your personal experiences. Abstract thinking has its place, but personal illustrations will help you and others remember the material more vividly.

3. Be open to others. Listen to the stories that other members tell, and respond to them in a way that does not invalidate their experiences.

Apply

1. Always ask yourself, "How can this apply to worship?"

2. Commit yourself to being a more intentional worshiper. Involve yourself in what is happening around you.

3. Determine your gifts. Ask yourself, "What can I do in worship that will minister to the body of Christ?" Then offer your gifts and talents to worship.

SUGGESTIONS FOR THE LEADER

Like the worship that it advocates, the group study in *Rediscovering the Missing Jewel* is dialogic in nature. Because this study has been developed around the principles of discussion and sharing, a monologue or lecture approach will not work. The following guidelines will help you encourage discussion, facilitate learning, and implement the practice of worship. Use these guidelines with "Part II: Group Discussion" in each session.

1. Encourage the participants to prepare thoroughly and to bring their Bibles and study guides to each session.

2. Begin each session with prayer. Since worship is a kind of prayer, learning about worship should be a prayerful experience.

3. Discuss each question individually. Ask for several answers and encourage people to react to comments made by others.

4. Use a chalkboard or flip chart or dry-erase board. Draw charts and symbols that visually enhance the ideas being presented. Outline major concepts.

5. Look for practical applications of answers and suggestions that are offered. Try asking questions like, "How would you include this in our worship?" "How would you feel about that change?" "How does this insight help you to be a better worshiper?"

6. Invite concrete personal illustrations. Ask questions like, "Have you experienced that? Where? When? Describe how you felt in that particular situation."

7. When you have concluded Session 9, send the names and addresses of all the students who will complete the class to: Institute for Worship Studies, Box 894, Wheaton, IL 60189. We will then send a certificate of accomplishment for each student in time for you to distribute them during the last class. The cost of each certificate is $1.00. (Add $3.00 for postage and handling.)

A WORD OF CAUTION

Of all the books in the Alleluia! series, *Rediscovering the Missing Jewel* may be for some the most difficult. In these lessons I have attempted to treat the worship of each historical period with academic integrity. For this reason the language and terms may sometimes be more difficult than you would wish. For example, the vocabulary of Eastern worship or Roman Catholic worship may seem foreign to a Protestant student. I considered trying to make the material simpler but finally decided that in this age of "dumbing down" worship, an alternative had to be offered. Being too simplistic about each tradition creates an unfair caricature.

If you become weary in these lessons, stick to them, because the reward of historical knowledge will be very satisfying. This should be the only book in this series for which such a warning is needed. You will find the vocabulary and terms of the other six books to be more generally familiar.

One final suggestion: Purchase the larger work upon which this course is based, volume 2 of *The Complete Library of Christian Worship*. This volume, entitled *Twenty Centuries of Christian Worship*, comprises a beautiful 8½-by-11-inch coffee table book that will inform your mind and inspire your heart through hours of reading and study.

PART I

THE BIBLICAL

FOUNDATIONS

OF CHRISTIAN

WORSHIP

OUR HEBREW ROOTS

A Study of Worship in Old Testament Times

 Most people in North America are not fond of history. Here and there, of course, you will find a history buff—someone here who loves to read about the early American settlers, someone there who is interested in the Native Americans, or someone else who has read everything there is about the Civil War.

In the 1970s when Alex Haley wrote his book, *Roots*, a lot of people who read the book or watched the television series became interested in the origins of this or that movement.

Consequently, a love of history grew among many people.

Some don't like history because of the way it was taught to them—facts, dry facts to be memorized. In this lesson we will study a lot more than facts. We will study how God worked among a living people, Israel, to bring salvation to the world. Our study is, you might say, a study in the history of salvation.

In worship we recall God's saving deeds, which were accomplished in history, and we anticipate the future—the new heavens and the new earth. For that reason it's important to know the history of God's saving deeds—the deeds of God that worship proclaims, recalls, and celebrates. Let's look at the history of the salvation that we celebrate in worship by studying how God initiated salvation with Abraham, Moses, and Christ.

ABRAHAM

When Adam and Eve (and all of us in them) fell away from God, God began to work in history to redeem and to restore us to fellowship. In worship we remember the saving deeds of God through which our relationship to God is restored. Our praise is directed to God, not to ourselves, because there is nothing we can do to save ourselves (Eph 2:8–10).

In worship we remember how God initiated a relationship with Abraham. Abraham was called to follow God in faith. As a result of Abraham's obedience, God entered into a covenant with him and promised to bless him as stated in Gen 12:1–3 (trans. Richard Leonard):

The Lord said to Abram, "Leave your country, your
people, and your father's household and go to the land
I will show you.
    I will make you into a great nation
        and I will bless you;
    I will make your name great,
        and you will be a blessing.
    I will bless those who bless you,
        and whoever curses you I will curse;
    and all peoples on earth
        will be blessed through you."

The worship of both Israel and the church is rooted in this promise. Both Jews and Christians regard Abraham as their "father in the faith." When Christians worship, we are mindful of Abraham because we believe that the blessing given to the whole world is the salvation that God offers to us all through Jesus Christ.

MOSES AND EXODUS

We all know the story of how Abraham's seed grew into the tribe of Israelites, how the Israelites were then held in bondage by Pharaoh, and how they called out to God from their cruel captivity, asking God to remember the covenant made with Abraham (Exod 2:23–25).

Cecil B. DeMille in his classic movie, *The Ten Commandments*, captured on screen the great drama of Israel's liberation from Egypt. We call this the Exodus event. In this event God delivered the people of Israel, made them a great nation, and entered into covenant with them at Mount Sinai.

By accepting this covenant, Israel agreed to be the people of God. The ceremony that established this covenant, which consisted of the people assembling before God at Mount Sinai for the reading of the Book of the Covenant and the ratification of the covenant with blood, was a worship event. From that moment on, Israel's worship would look back to this as the historic event that they would continually proclaim, recall, and celebrate. (For a study of the worship character of this event, see Exod 24:1–8.)

By accepting this covenant, the people of Israel agreed to obey and to worship God. Consequently, God gave them the Ten Commandments to live by and the tabernacle to worship in (Exod 25–31).

Israel has become the people of God's saving event—the Exodus.

This event will always stand at the center of Israelite worship. Israel will recall and enact this event when it celebrates the Passover and when it presents sacrifices to God at the tabernacle and later at the temple.

THE CHRIST EVENT

Christians believe the Exodus event is a type of God's saving action in Jesus Christ.

- Just as Israel was in bondage to Pharaoh, so all people are in bondage to the power of evil (Eph 2:2).
- Just as God sent Moses to deliver Israel from their bondage, so God sent Jesus to deliver us from our sins (Matt 1:21).
- Just as God entered into a covenant with Israel, so God enters into covenant with the church (Heb 8:8–12).
- Just as God established a tabernacle with a high priest for worship, so God established a new high priest and an entrance into the Holy of Holies through Jesus Christ (Heb 9:11–14).
- Just as the tabernacle was characterized by sacrifices, so the new covenant is characterized by the once-for-all sacrifice of Jesus Christ (Heb 10:15–18).
- Just as Israel looked forward to the promised land, so Christians hope for the new heavens and the new earth (Rev 21:1).

CONCLUSION

In this lesson we have recognized the simple but profound truth that worship proclaims, recalls, and celebrates God's saving events. We have focused on the two great saving deeds of God that define the worship of Israel and the worship of the church.

Israel is the people of the Exodus event. Their history and their worship hearken back to this event.

Christians are the people of the Christ event. Their history and their worship hearken back to this event.

Today in worship God's people celebrate God's saving events and in so doing bring praise, glory, and honor to God.

STUDY GUIDE

Read Session 1, "Our Hebrew Roots," before starting the study guide.

PART I: PERSONAL STUDY

Complete the following questions individually.

1. *Life Connection*

- Remember a history course that you took in either high school or college. Was this course (a) a memorization of facts—dates, places, and people or (b) a study of trends, shifts in power, development of ideas? What was your response to the course? _____

_____

_____

_____

_____

_____

2. *Content Questions*

- What do we do in worship? _____

_____

_____

_____

- What is the blessing given to the whole world that worship remembers?

_____

_____

_____

_____

- What aspects of the covenant between God and Abraham were fulfilled in the Exodus event? _____

_____

_____

_____

- Read Exodus 24:1–8. What elements of worship do you find in the covenant agreement made between God and Israel? _____

  _____

  _____

  _____

- Explain how this event—the Exodus, and the covenant at Mount Sinai—will always stand at the center of Israel's worship. _____

  _____

  _____

  _____

  _____

- What is the saving event of the New Testament? _____

  _____

  _____

  _____

- Draw a picture or graph that compares Old Testament worship with New Testament worship.

3. *Application*

- Think about a recent worship service in your church. How were the events of the living, dying, rising, and coming again of Christ proclaimed, enacted, or celebrated in Scripture, sermon, song, or prayer during the service? (You may want to glance over a recent church bulletin to refresh your memory.)

PART II. GROUP DISCUSSION

The following questions are designed for group discussion.

1. *Life Connection*

♦ Begin by asking several members of the class to tell stories about history classes in high school or college. Then ask, "What is your impression of the approach toward the history of worship in this course, *Rediscovering the Missing Jewel?*"

2. *Thought Questions*

♦ Many people define worship as "giving honor to God." This lesson expands on that definition, saying that worship is a recitation of God's saving deeds that brings God's saving action to the worshiping community through proclamation, enactment, and celebration. How does this view expand your understanding of worship? Write your answers on the board.

♦ Read Exodus 24:1–8 together and answer the following questions:

What elements of worship do you find in this passage?

In what way are these elements of worship a recitation of God's saving work in the Exodus event?

What do you think the people of Israel experienced in this worship?

What parallels, if any, do you find between the Exodus event and the worship of your church?

Develop an order of service from this text.

♦ Compare the worship of Israel and the worship of the church. Put two columns on the board. Put Israel on the left and the church on the right. Drawing from the text, identify parallels between the two. Ask, "How is the Exodus event a type of God's saving action in the New Testament? What does this say to us about Christian worship?"

3. *Application*

◆ Review a recent worship and answer the following questions. (You may want to consult a church bulletin or whatever service material your group uses.)

◆ What act of worship was directed toward "honoring God's worth"?

◆ What act or acts of worship proclaimed, enacted, or celebrated God's saving events?

◆ Was the worship a narrative of God's saving action or was it a program?

◆ What did you learn in this lesson that: (1) strengthens your understanding of worship? (2) you would like to see added to the worship of your local church?

Our Christian Roots

A Study of Worship in New Testament Times

 When I first became interested in worship and worship renewal more than twenty years ago, I became involved in a house church. I resonated to this house church worship because it was casual and intimate, unlike the worship of the larger church in its auditorium-like sanctuary. The small group intimacy and the friendly atmosphere of a lived-in home led me to feel a kinship with the early church, which met for worship in houses.

While early Christians continued to meet in the temple courts for daily prayer (Acts 2:46) and more than likely in the synagogues, their primary place of meeting was the home.

House Church Worship in New Testament Times

The clearest picture we have of house church worship comes from Acts 2:42–47. Some of the elements that characterize our worship today were first experienced in the house church worship of Jerusalem. We know from the description in Acts 2 that early Christian worship included the following:

- apostolic teaching
- fellowship
- breaking of bread
- prayer
- the experience of awe
- wonders and miraculous signs
- the experience of community
- caring for the needs of others
- eating together
- the experience of gladness
- the experience of growth

Scholars suggest that early Christian worship met in the context of an agape feast, a full-blown meal in which all of the acts of worship listed above took place (*agapē* means "love").

Imagine yourself in the first century. When you assemble with other Christians for worship, you go to someone's home and eat a full meal. In the context of a joyous meal, you hear stories about Jesus and apply them to your own life. You break bread, anticipating that the Jesus who broke bread with his disciples will be present with you, even as he was present on the road to Emmaus and in the upper room. You engage in fellowship with your friends, meet new people, hold up each other's concerns in prayer, and give money and assistance to those in need. In that context your heart is full of joy and gladness.

While house church worship is clearly present in the New Testament, we are also able to identify another style of worship called body life worship.

BODY LIFE WORSHIP IN THE EARLY CHURCH

In recent years there has been a great deal of talk about rediscovering the body-like nature of the church. I like this metaphor because the rediscovery of the church as a body is essential to renewal in the local church.

It is interesting that Paul held up the image of the body to the Corinthian church in particular.

The image of the body was presented to the Corinthians as a corrective to their divisiveness. When you read the First Letter to the Corinthians, particularly chapter 3, you get the feeling that these people were divisive, even competitive. These qualities spilled over into the worship of the church. Paul had to say "Look! Don't compete with each other in worship. Remember that you are a body. A body has many parts that function in harmony."

This message is particularly clear in 1 Corinthians 12, where Paul gives the following instructions about how to be a good worshiping community:

+ When we say "Jesus is Lord" in worship, we do so by the Holy Spirit.
+ Each of us brings a different gift to worship.
+ Each gift is for the common good, including
    wisdom
    knowledge
    faith
    healing
    miraculous powers

prophecy
discernment
tongues
interpretation of tongues
- All these gifts come from one and the same Spirit.

The recovery of body life is an indispensable feature of worship renewal. I recently visited a number of churches known for their renewal of worship and discovered that in each one of these churches there was a commitment to discern each other's gifts. I also discovered the willingness of the people—the priesthood of all believers—to put their gifts to work.

In addition to house church worship and body life worship, the New Testament clearly indicates liturgical worship.

LITURGICAL WORSHIP IN THE EARLY CHURCH

I grew up in the free church tradition. This tradition boasts of its freedom in worship, everyone seeming anxious to say, "I'm not liturgical!"

The word "liturgical" comes from the Greek word *leitourgia*, which means "the work of the people." The work of the people is to proclaim, to enact, and to celebrate the living, dying, and rising of Christ. Through this work he overthrows the powers of evil. Because all traditions—liturgical, free church, and charismatic—do that work in their worship, it is appropriate to say they all have a liturgy (work).

But the word "liturgy" has come to mean something additional. It now refers to a set order that includes written prayer, ceremonial vestments, and ornate space. So someone who says, "I'm not liturgical," is expressing a preference for worship that is simple and plain.

It is a matter of interest to note that the New Testament describes a very plain worship (Acts 2:42–47) and a highly ornate worship as well (read Rev 4–5 looking for liturgical elements of worship). You may want to read through the entire book of Revelation to study the worship it describes. Some scholars argue that the worship described in Revelation influenced the liturgical worship of the Eastern churches. Here is a summary of those influences:
- The Throne (Rev 4:2): This is a symbol of the presence of God. In Eastern churches the holy table is the throne of the Most High.
- Pantocrator (Rev 1:8): In Eastern churches frescoes of Christ that are located in the center dome symbolize Christ's reign over the whole universe.

- Lamb of God (Rev 5:6): The Lamb of God who takes away the sin of the world is also the heavenly high priest.
- Twenty-four Elders (Rev 4:4, 10): This image forms the basis of the elders, a semicircle of presbyters that surrounds the holy table during the celebration of the divine liturgy.
- The White Robe (Rev 19:1–8): The alb or white robe worn by the Orthodox priest is a symbol of all who are clothed with Christ.
- The Celestial Court (Rev 4:1–6): This is a concrete image of Eastern court liturgy—worship.
- The Martyrs (Rev 6:9): The sacrifice of the martyrs, which is associated with Christ, has always held an important place in Eastern worship.
- Hymns (Rev 11:17–18; 15:3–4): Segments of these hymns are found in the liturgies of the east.
- Doxologies (Rev 1:6; 4:11; 5:12, 13): These doxologies are used in Eastern worship.
- Amen (Rev 5:14; 19:14; 22:20): In the Eastern Orthodox liturgy the "Amen" is sung frequently.
- Alleluia (Rev 19:1, 3–4, 6): The "Alleluia" appears frequently in the Eastern liturgy.
- The Wedding (Rev 19:6–8): The image of the great supper of the messianic banquet is expressed in Holy Communion.

CONCLUSION

In the New Testament we find three pictures of worship relating to three broad traditions of worship that are being continued in the contemporary church. I find myself asking, "What does that mean for my attitude toward worship?" I find myself affirming elements in all the traditions and recognizing that God may be worshiped in more than one style.

God is honored and praised in house church worship, body life worship, and liturgical worship.

STUDY GUIDE

Read Session 2, "Our Christian Roots," before starting the study guide.

PART I: PERSONAL STUDY

Complete the following questions individually.

1. *Life Connection*

◆ This lesson illustrates three kinds of New Testament worship—house church worship, body life worship, and liturgical worship. Describe your own experience of one or more of these worship services, including one that is *unlike* the worship of your local church. _____

_____

_____

_____

_____

2. *Content Questions*

◆ An early house church worship experience is described in Acts 2:42–47. The terms listed below summarize that service. After each item write a corresponding experience that you have had in worship.

Apostolic teaching _____
Fellowship _____
Breaking of bread _____
Prayer _____
The experience of awe _____
Wonders and miraculous signs _____
The experience of community _____
Caring for the needs of others _____
Eating together _____
The experience of gladness _____
The experience of growth _____

◆ A body life worship in the early church is described in 1 Cor 12. The terms listed below summarize that experience. After each item write a corresponding worship experience that you have had.

Proclaiming "Jesus is Lord" _____

Each bringing a different gift to worship: _____

Wisdom _____

Knowledge _____

Faith_____

Healing _____

Miraculous powers_____

Prophecy _____

Discernment _____

Tongues _____

Interpretation of tongues _____

◆ Liturgical worship is described in the book of Revelation, particularly chapters 4–5. Read that passage and then list all the elements of worship associated with liturgical churches. _____

_____

_____

_____

_____

_____

_____

◆ Take time to think about these three New Testament approaches to worship. What do they tell you about the variety of worship that exists in today's church?

_____

_____

_____

_____

PART II. GROUP DISCUSSION

The following questions are designed for group discussion.

1. *Life Connection*
- Begin your discussion by asking group members to describe experiences they have had in connection with house church worship, body life worship, and liturgical worship.

2. *Thought Questions*
- Walk through each content question in Part 1, the individual study. Take notes on the board as you discuss the three types of worship in the New Testament.
- The principles of Christian worship include the following:

   (1)   The proclamation and enactment of the living, the dying, and the rising of Christ

   (2)   An experience of divine action from above

   (3)   An experience of human response, such as song, prayer, witness, joy, etc. Review the three types of New Testament worship and identify examples of the three principles of worship at work in each.

- Someone has said that there is ony one kind of worship, gospel worship, but there are many styles of worship. What do you think about this?
- What does each style of worship bring to the others?

3. *Application*
- Which style of worship is closest to your local church?
- Which style of worship would this group find most threatening?
- Does the worship of your local church incorporate elements of worship from more than one of these styles? Which ones?
- What would a worship incorporating all three styles look like? Brainstorm this question and put your answers on the board.
- How would you go about introducing a blend of traditional and contemporary worship ("convergence worship") in your church?

PART II

❧❧❧❧

WORSHIP FROM THE TIME OF THE EARLY CHURCH THROUGH THE NINETEENTH CENTURY

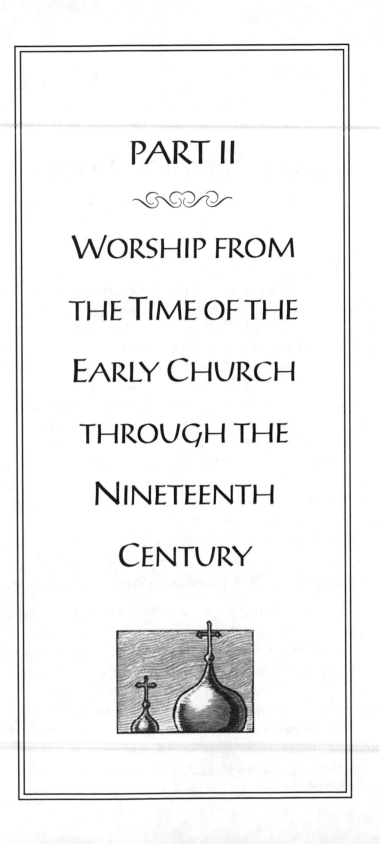

OUR COMMON ROOTS

A Study in the Worship of the Early Church

 In Session 2, I mentioned a house church that I attended more than twenty years ago. Today the house church movement is growing throughout the world. The members of many large local churches meet during the week in small cell groups that can properly be called house churches.

A passion I experienced as a member of the house church, one that I still have today, is to share what the early Christians experienced in their worship.

In the house church that met in my home, we always took time to read and study the Word, pray for each other's needs, sing, celebrate Communion, enjoy a full meal together, and spend most of Sunday afternoon enjoying each other's company.

These acts of worship were modeled on our understanding of the house church worship in the early centuries of the faith (larger buildings for worship were not used until after the conversion of the emperor Constantine in the fourth century).

In this lesson we are going to study the house church worship of the second century as described by Justin Martyr.

BACKGROUND TO JUSTIN MARTYR AND SECOND-CENTURY WORSHIP

Justin Martyr was a Christian teacher in Rome who was martyred, along with several of his students, in the mid-second century. His *First Apology* (the word means "defense") was addressed to the household of the non-Christian emperor Antoninus Pius. It defended the new faith and argued for conversion to Christianity.

In chapters 61–67 Justin describes aspects of Christian worship, primarily to explain to non-Christians that the worship services were neither orgies nor cannibalistic rites, two accusations leveled against early Christians. He carefully avoids terminology used in pagan worship, such as the term "priest," and strives to convince his readers that the Christians who gather in the liturgy are morally upright and responsible citizens. In the course of his description, Justin preserves a picture of second-century worship in Rome in his Greek-speaking community. His weekly liturgy is composed of a reading service together with a celebration of the Eucharist, the first clear indication of this combination.

JUSTIN MARTYR'S DESCRIPTION OF WORSHIP

In *Twenty Centuries of Christian Worship*, scholar Lizette Larson-Miller discusses Justin Martyr's description of second-century worship.

INTRODUCTION

The community of believers that has gathered in the home of Justin the Teacher is one of several small Christian communities spread throughout the city of Rome. The small communities may know about each other, but they worship in individual groups that are based on family connections, language, and nationality, or on their relationship to the teacher who first communicated to them the gospel of Jesus the Christ. Most of those gathering on this Sunday evening speak Greek, and many of them are recent immigrants from the regions of Cappadocia, Palestine, and Samaria, like their teacher, Justin.

The choice of Sunday for a meeting day is no accident; Justin himself teaches that Sunday has a double significance: It is the "first day, on which God transformed darkness and made the universe," and it is also the day on which "Jesus Christ our Savior rose from the dead." These Christians gather to celebrate both of those divine events, remembering the blessings of creation, as they did in their Jewish childhood, and the death and resurrection of Jesus, which made all creation new.

When the workday has ended for the Christians, they gather quietly at the home of Justin, who lives above a shopkeeper named Martinus in a typical Roman apartment building. With living quarters as close as they are in Rome, the comings and goings of Justin's students, as well as the weekly gatherings for liturgy, cannot be a secret to the neighbors. In their very act of gathering, the Christians are risking arrest and possibly death.

SCRIPTURE READINGS

Worship begins with readings from Scripture—the Law and the Prophets of the Hebrew Bible—or from the recently circulated accounts of Jesus' death and resurrection that have been passed on through the followers of Jesus' disciples. Listening to the stories from Scripture that they grew up with, many in the community remember their Jewish roots and feel at home. The stories from Scripture are new and unusual to the Greek members, who have grown up with stories of Greek and Roman gods. The explanation that always follows the reading is helpful to their understanding.

As the teacher of the community, Justin is responsible to keep the rolls on which the Scriptures are written and to gather the stories of Jesus and the letters between Christian communities. This Sunday gathering meets in his house because he is the keeper of the books and has the room to store them. The reader chosen for the day reads from Justin's collection, standing at an upright table with an assistant who helps handle the rolls of Scripture. When the readings are finished (when the president signals that he has heard enough!), the president—one of the elders of the community—begins to explain them. First he interprets the readings from the Hebrew Scripture with regard to the prophecies of Christ and their fulfillment in Jesus, then he applies this interpretation and the stories of Jesus to the lives of the gathered Christians.

The president does not have the training and education of a catechist (instructor in church doctrine) like Justin. But he can share his experience of surviving persecution and imprisonment and the wisdom he has gained through living a life in imitation of Christ.

Prayer

In response to the inspiring words of the president who urges each person to imitate the acts of Jesus in his or her life, the community rises from the floor, which is spread with rugs, to offer prayers. Standing with uplifted hands, they pray as a baptized community, confident that their prayers for the world and for the wider church are heard by the gracious God referred to in their readings. In their prayers they remember especially those of their own community who are sick or dying, as well as the two members who have been arrested for professing Christ, betrayed by non-Christian family members.

The Kiss of Peace

After the prayers are completed, all of the baptized Christians acknowledge the presence of the Spirit in each other by sharing a kiss, which signifies the presence of God's Spirit in each person. It is this kiss—exchanged on the lips because it is identified with the breath of God in the creation stories—that has so scandalized the critics of Christianity and has led to stories that Christians gather to conduct orgies. For the Christians, however, the kiss is not a scandal, but a sign of the pure love of God. It is a physical expression of unity as the community moves toward sharing Holy Communion.

BREAD AND WINE

Certain members of the community have brought bread and wine for the Eucharist. (By the second century, Communion was called "Eucharist," a word that means "thanks." The early Christians gave eucharist—thanks—for the bread and wine.) As the exchange of the kiss of peace is completed, the freshly baked bread and homemade wine are brought to a table in the front of the room. A pitcher of water is brought from the back so that the strong red wine of the Roman countryside can be diluted.

After the plate and the cup have been arranged on the table, the same leader who conducted the readings offers a prayer of thanksgiving to God for the gifts that have been given to all those present. Chanting in the style associated with reciting epic poems, the president recounts the works of God for which God is being blessed, including the central act of sending the Son of God for the salvation of all. Following a structure inherited from Jewish tradition, the president thanks God in his own words and asks the Spirit of God to come down on all who are gathered in the room. At the conclusion of his chanting, the community adds its assent to all that had been said by singing "Amen" ("so be it"), one of several Hebrew words that these Greek-speaking Christians have borrowed.

BREAD AND WINE RECEIVED AND SENT TO ABSENT MEMBERS

When the prayer of thanksgiving ends, all the people come forward to receive the consecrated bread and wine, gathering around the deacons who supervise the distribution. After all receive a small chunk of bread and drink from the single large cup, the remaining bread and wine are given to the two deacons who take it to members of the community who are sick, as well as to the ones who are awaiting martyrdom in prison. The very act of gathering the remaining bread and wine and watching the president bless the two deacons as they go on their way reminds all those present of how very close the threat of arrest is to them and how precious is this time together.

CONTRIBUTIONS AND CARE FOR THE POOR

As the members of this small community prepare to leave, those who have extra clothing, food, or money give it to the president to distribute as needed. They know that these gifts are a matter of life and death for some. (In that society there were few nets to catch those unable to feed themselves.) As the gifts are brought up to the president, he gently acknowledges each person, proud that the prayer offered by the community has yielded such tangible fruit.

After bidding farewell to each other, the members of the community return to their own homes. Some return to servants' quarters in elaborate palaces, some to family homes filled with nonbelievers, and others to humble dwellings on the outskirts of Rome. All leave praying that everyone will remain safe until the next Sunday when they will gather once again with their new family, born in baptism and sustained by the Word and the Eucharist.

CONCLUSION

These insights into early Christian worship show that worship was much more than a ritual for second-century Christians. For them, worship was a matter of life. Worship defined life and sustained life in a hostile culture.

Modern culture is becoming increasingly hostile to the Christian faith and to its values. We can learn how to function in a hostile society from that band of early Christians who worked and worshiped in the secular, pagan society of the Roman Empire.

The material of this chapter is adapted from Lizette Larson-Miller, "Justin Martyr: The *First Apology*," in *Twenty Centuries of Christian Worship* (Hendrickson, 1994), pp. 148–50.

STUDY GUIDE

Read Session 3, "Our Common Roots," before starting the study guide.

PART I: PERSONAL STUDY

Complete the following questions individually.

1. *Life Connection*

♦ Most of us either have met a person from a country where Christians are under persecution or read an article about Christians who live in such a country (e.g., the People's Republic of China). Because this lesson deals with worship in second-century Rome, where Christians were persecuted and put to death for their faith, you can get in touch with this era best by remembering a story of Christian persecution in recent times. Write about a true story that you have heard or write an imaginative account of how it would feel to attend a worship service when it could result in death. _____

_____

_____

_____

_____

_____

2. *Content Questions*

♦ What two accusations were leveled against Christian worship by the Roman government? _____

_____

_____

_____

♦ What two parts of Christian worship does Justin describe? _____

_____

_____

_____

- Why did the Christians worship on Sunday? _____
  _____
  _____
  _____
  _____

- Where did they meet for worship? _____
  _____
  _____
  _____
  _____

- What readings did they hear in worship? _____
  _____
  _____
  _____
  _____

- What posture did these Christians assume when they prayed? _____
  _____
  _____
  _____
  _____

- What was the meaning of the kiss of peace? _____
  _____
  _____
  _____

- What is the meaning of the word "Eucharist"? _____
  _____
  _____
  _____

- How often did the early Christians celebrate the Eucharist?_____

_____

_____

- What was the content of the prayer over the bread and wine?_____

_____

_____

_____

_____

_____

- How did the people receive the bread and wine?_____

_____

_____

_____

_____

- Describe the character and substance of the offerings made by the early Christians.

_____

_____

_____

_____

_____

3. *Application*

- How does the worship of your church differ from the worship of the second-century church described by Justin? How would you describe the worship of your church to a person who knows little about Christianity? Write out your description. _____

_____

_____

_____

_____

_____

PART II: GROUP DISCUSSION

The following questions are designed for group discussion.

1. *Life Connection*

+ Begin your discussion by asking various members to tell stories about worship in countries where Christians are persecuted. How do these stories help you appreciate the worship circumstances of the second century?

2. *Thought Questions*

+ What do you think a second-century Christian actually experienced in worship?

+ How may second-century worship, as described by Justin, have differed from first-century worship? In what ways may it have been the same?

+ If a second-century worshiper were to visit your church, what changes in worship would he or she point to? What would be familiar?

+ Compare first-century worship, second-century worship, and modern worship. Put three columns on the board, listing under each those characteristics that best describe the order and content.

3. *Application*

+ Identify three elements of early Christian worship that you would like to see incorporated into the worship of your church. Have students offer suggestions and write them all on the board. Then decide which three are most important and why. Finally, discuss how you would incorporate these elements into your own worship.

VISUALIZING FAITH IN WORSHIP
A Study in Eastern Orthodox Worship

 I grew up in the free church tradition of worship, which traces its roots to the Puritans. While most free church communities no longer worship as their Puritan fathers and mothers did, they retain some of the convictions of Puritan worship.

One primary conviction of Puritan worship is that Christians are to be plain in their worship. This concept of being "plain" extends to every aspect of worship, including plain and direct speech, plain dress (as opposed to vestment), plain and simple music, and a plain setting for worship.

Puritans and those who followed them interpreted New Testament worship and the teaching of Jesus about worship (and life in general) as promoting simplicity and plainness. They believed that the ceremonials of the Old Testament temple, with all of their beauty and sacred ritual, ministry and festivals, had been done away with. I came to Orthodox worship out of this perspective.

You can imagine my own first impression of Orthodox worship. I missed its heart and saw it as pure ritualism.

Orthodox Christians follow the beauty and ceremonials of worship described in Rev 4–5. Once I understood this conviction, I wanted to see Orthodox worship as Orthodox Christians see it, not judging it from the Puritan influence in my worship tradition.

While worship is thought to have been relatively plain during the first three centuries of the Christian church, it became considerably more ceremonial and dramatic after the conversion of Constantine. In Byzantium (the eastern part of the Roman world) the church visualized the gospel in its worship. It celebrated Christ through the architecture of the building and through the use of vestments, icons, and frescoes. Session 4 looks at this visualization of worship and seeks to appreciate an aesthetic approach to worship. (Students who have never been in an Eastern Orthodox church may want to visit a local Orthodox church in connection with the study. Actually seeing what we will be describing will enhance their under-standing of the material of this session immeasurably.)

THE WORSHIP BUILDING: AN ICON OF THE KINGDOM OF GOD

In his chapter in *Twenty Centuries of Christian Worship,* scholar and Orthodox priest John Warren Morris describes Orthodox worship. The following discussion draws from his work.

A central feature of Eastern worship is a commitment to make earthly worship follow the pattern of heavenly worship (see Rev 4–5). This passion to divinize earthly worship extends to the creation of a heavenlike worship space.

For example, in Constantinople ecclesiastical architecture reached its highest development in Hagia Sophia, the Church of the Holy Wisdom, built by the emperor Justinian in the sixth century. A vast domed structure, the Church of Holy Wisdom set the pattern for all subsequent churches in the Eastern Church. There were no pews, only a few seats for the elderly and the infirm.

Believers in ancient Byzantium considered the church building an image (icon) of the kingdom of God, the dome representing the vault of the heavens. The image of Christ the Almighty (Pantocrator) located in the dome symbolized Christ ruling over the universe. The mosaics and paintings portrayed the saints and the entire company of heaven, which mystically joined the faithful for the celebration of the Eucharist. The barrier between the nave and the sanctuary symbolized the mystery of the Eucharist and the division between heaven and earth. The holy table, at the center of the sanctuary, represented the throne of God in heaven.

THE SYMBOLIC MEANING OF THE WORSHIP LEADERS

Today in free church worship the worship leaders do not assume any symbolic meaning. They stand before the congregation and lead worship, inspiring others to worship with all their hearts, but they do not represent biblical images or symbols in any visual way. This was not the case in Byzantine worship. Here the people who held positions of leadership were laden with meaning, as were the clothing they wore and the actions they took. Those who developed Eastern worship desired to make the leaders of earthly worship into the image of the leaders of heavenly worship (see Rev 4–5). The following list summarizes this symbolism and imagery:

- The bishop symbolized Christ, the true minister of the Sacrament.
- Priests symbolized the twelve apostles.
- Deacons symbolized the ministers of heaven.

- Altar servers symbolized the angels of heaven.
- Clerical robes symbolized several elements from the gospel:

  The inner gown symbolized the robe of baptism.

  The stole (worn over the inner gown) signified the robe of Aaron and the cloth by which Christ was tied as he was taken to the cross.

  The cape symbolized the cross carried by Christ to his death.

- The bishop wore a large woolen stole wrapped over his neck as a shepherd wrapped a wounded lamb around his neck and carried it to safety.
- Deacons wore a thin stole that represented the wings of angels.
- The clergy symbolized Christ standing before the throne of God, while the deacons symbolized the angels who act as messengers between heaven and earth.

The Symbolic Meaning of the Liturgy

The liturgy of the Eastern Orthodox Church, like the space in which it takes place and like its leaders of worship, is highly symbolic. Eastern Christians believe that words themselves are symbols, not mere empty letters. Consequently, the language of the liturgy is pictorial, poetic, and lavish. It is modeled after the lavish nature of the language of heavenly worship.

An example of the Eastern language of worship is found in the prefatory prayer to the Eucharist from the St. John Chrysostom Liturgy, a liturgy that traces its origin to the fourth century. Below is that prayer. Observe the poetic and imagistic nature of its elusive language.

The Anaphora

The priest says: The grace of our Lord Jesus Christ, and the love of the God and Father, and the fellowship of the Holy Spirit be with you all.
People: And with your spirit.
Priest: Let us lift up our hearts.
People: We have them with the Lord.
Priest: Let us give thanks to the Lord.
People: It is fitting and right to worship the Father, the Son, and the Holy Spirit, the consubstantial and undivided Trinity.

The priest begins the holy anaphora: It is fitting and right to hymn you, bless you, to praise you, to give you thanks, to worship you in all places of your dominion. For you are God, ineffable, inconceivable, invisible, incomprehensible, existing always and in the same way, you and your only-begotten Son and your Holy Spirit. You brought us out of not-being to being; and when we had fallen, you raised us up again; and did not cease to do everything until you had brought us up to heaven, and granted us the kingdom that is to come. For all these things we give thanks to you and your only-begotten Son and to your Holy Spirit, for all that we know and do not know, your seen and unseen benefits that have come upon us. We give you thanks also for this ministry; vouchsafe to receive it from our hands, even though thousands of archangels and ten thousands of angels stand before you, cherubim and seraphim, with six wings and many eyes, flying on high *(aloud)* singing the triumphal hymn proclaiming, crying, and saying:

People: Holy, holy, holy, Lord of Sabaoth; heaven and earth are full of your glory. Hosanna in the highest. Blessed is he who comes in the name of the Lord. Hosanna in the highest.

CONCLUSION

For many worshipers the worship language and imagery of the Eastern Orthodox Church is foreign territory, although recently Catholic Christians and Protestant Christians have gained a new appreciation for the Eastern Church and its ways.

There is much to be learned from the Eastern Church. If our worship does join heavenly worship as the book of Revelation attests, then we need to be more mindful of how the words we use and how the setting in which worship takes place help us achieve the sense of being in the very presence of God, worshiping the one who is high and holy and lifted up above all others.

The material in this chapter is adapted from John Warren Morris, "The Byzantine Liturgy," in *Twenty Centuries of Christian Worship* (Hendrickson, 1994), pp. 152–71.

Read Session 4, "Visualizing Faith in Worship," before starting the study guide.

PART I PERSONAL STUDY

Complete the following questions individually.

1. *Life Connection*

◆ For those who have never witnessed an Eastern Orthodox liturgy, I suggest that you attend a service in order to gain a full appreciation of this liturgy. If you are unable to visit an Orthodox church, do one of the following. (1) Go to the library and find a book on Russian architecture. It will be filled with churches, showing both the exteriors and the interiors. (2) Recall your feelings at seeing an Orthodox church, either one on television or one in your neighborhood. Write out your impression of Orthodox architecture. _____

_____

_____

_____

_____

_____

_____

2. *Content Questions*

◆ Read Rev 4–5. List every visual image that you find in these two chapters. _____

_____

_____

_____

_____

_____

_____

- Reread the section entitled "The Worship Building: An Icon of the Kingdom of God." Explain how the interior of the Orthodox churches reflects the heavens. _____

_____

_____

_____

_____

- Reread "The Symbolic Meaning of the Worship Leaders," then reread Rev 4:1–11. How does this passage help you appreciate the symbolic character of Orthodox worship? _____

_____

_____

_____

_____

- Reread "The Symbolic Meaning of the Liturgy." Read Isa 6:1–6. Then write out all the words and phrases you find in the anaphora prayer that capture the transcendence of God. _____

_____

_____

_____

_____

3. *Application*

- There is a saying, "We shape our environment and then our environment shapes us." How is this saying true of the environment of the worship space in your church? _____

_____

_____

_____

_____

PART II. GROUP DISCUSSION

The following questions are designed for group discussion.

1. *Life Connection*

◆ Begin your study by asking group members to report on their visit to an Orthodox church, on their study in the library, or on their response to the architecture of the Eastern Church. Ask, "How does the architecture of the Eastern Church visualize the Christian faith?"

2. *Thought Questions*

◆ Does Rev 4–5 simply describe visual worship, or does it prescribe visual worship as normative?

◆ Why do you think that the Puritans insisted on plain churches?

◆ Should our church interiors be plain, without any visualization of the faith, or should they visualize the faith? Why?

◆ Compare the interior of the Orthodox church to the interior of your church.

◆ Compare your visual image of the Orthodox clergy leading worship to the sight of worship leaders of your church.

◆ Compare the word picture in Isa 6:1–6 with the word pictures of God that are used in your worship.

3. *Application*

◆ What arguments would you give to support a transcendent space? It may be said that the architecture of the Eastern Church represents divine transcendence (God above), while the architecture of many contemporary churches represents the Incarnation (God among us). Is the architecture of your church a transcendent or an incarnational architecture?

◆ What arguments would you give to support an incarnational space? What would you need to do to your worship space to achieve a balance of both the transcendence of God and the incarnation of God?

DRAMATIZING THE FAITH IN WORSHIP

A Study in Roman Catholic Worship

Like most Protestants from the free church tradition, I grew up with a certain fear of the Roman Catholic Church. I was told that their faith and worship amounted to external ritualism and that true faith was not to be found in a Catholic heart.

My first real contact with Roman Catholics occurred when I was a graduate student at Concordia Theological Seminary in St. Louis. One of my teachers invited me to become a member of a prayer fellowship group that included several Roman Catholic priests and seminary students from St. Louis University. Because of my prejudice against Catholics, I wasn't sure I wanted to join the group. However, I felt shamed by my attitude when I discovered the deep spirituality possessed by the Roman Catholic priests and seminary students in this group. I was stunned to discover the depth of their prayer life and the breadth of their understanding of Scripture. Although that group met for only two years, it made a profound impact on my life, causing me to realize how much spiritual depth can be found in the Catholic tradition.

Three years later on an Easter weekend, I found myself walking into a Catholic Church for the great paschal vigil service (a service on the Saturday night before Easter Sunday whose origins go back to the third century).

I opened the door and was astonished to find the vestibule in total darkness. Although I could not see them, I knew the vestibule was full of people because I could hear them breathing, and I could sense that some of them were moving around. I stood still and waited to see what would happen.

All of a sudden, flames from the center of the room soared several feet into the air, lighting up the whole room. In that same moment the priest sang out with great joy, "The light of Christ," to which the entire congregation responded, "Thanks be to God." What followed was one of the most powerful, life-changing liturgies of high drama that I had ever experienced in my life.

THE MASS AS HIGH DRAMA

The scene I just described is one of several worship experiences that set me on a journey to find out what worship is all about and why it has made such an impact on my life. I began to search for the missing jewel in my own life.

As I continued my search, I realized that one of the polarities of worship is intimacy versus theater. (I am using "theater" to refer to a more dramatic style of worship.)

Thinking about early Christian worship and studying its style of worship, I came to realize that it is characterized by intimacy. For example, you can't read Acts 2:42–47 without getting a sense of the intimacy that those early Christians must have experienced in their worship: a sense of community, mutual love, concern for each other's needs. Reading and studying this passage makes me want to run out and find that community because it presents a warm and welcoming God.

When I turn to the book of Revelation (chapters 4–5), I'm impressed by the theater of worship. I see a throne with God seated on it and surrounded by myriad angels, with the cherubim and the seraphim, Michael and all the archangels, crying, singing aloud, and shouting, "Holy, holy, holy, Lord God of Sabaoth, the whole earth is full of your glory."

In this theater I don't think about myself and my needs. My attention is drawn to God. I worship God in God's transcendence and holiness. I see God high and holy and lifted up, and I want to fall before God as Isaiah did, acknowledging my own unworthiness.

Ancient worship—the liturgical worship of both the Byzantine Church and the Roman Catholic Church—was given to theater. It was high drama, like the drama in Revelation.

Catholic worship in the Middle Ages was like the heavenly worship described in Revelation. It was high drama. But unlike the drama of heavenly worship, which involves everyone, medieval drama was worship that you watched. The people themselves were not participants. The great drama was played out in the front of the church, with the celebrant, the deacons, the acolytes, and the choir playing their parts (as in Rev 4–5). The congregation stood to watch the drama as an act of devotion to the Lord.

Roman Catholic worship became the spectacular dramatic production of the Christian faith. Consequently, great attention was paid to every part of the ritual—all of which came to mean something particular from the life of Christ. While we now know that this interpretation was imposed on the liturgy, it did provide a historic panorama of the life, death, and resurrection of Christ for an illiterate people. Most people could not read the Gospels, so they depended on their ability to watch and to hear as the means by which the gospel story was communicated to them.

This medieval Roman Mass consisted of four main parts: the Mass of the catechumens (persons being instructed in the faith and preparing for baptism), the offertory (offering the bread and wine), the canon (the prayers of thanksgiving over the bread and wine), and the Communion (the reception of bread and wine by the priest).

As you read about the Roman Mass in the following description, try to imagine yourself in a large medieval cathedral experiencing the drama of the unfolding Mass.

THE MASS OF THE CATECHUMENS

Ascending to the altar, which is usually elevated by a few steps, the priest places the covered chalice and paten (vessels for wine and bread) on a linen cloth called the corporal at the center of the altar in front of the tabernacle. The entire liturgy will be celebrated with the priest's back to the people.

After kissing the altar, the priest proceeds to the right side (epistle side) and reads the introit (opening psalm of worship).

After the reading the priest returns to the middle of the lowest altar step, where he and the servers (acolytes) say the prayers at the foot of the altar. These prayers include the double confession and the ninefold kyrie eleison ("Lord have mercy" said or sung nine times).

The opening rites are punctuated with numerous genuflections and altar kissings as prescribed by the rubrics of the missal (the book containing that which is said or sung at Mass).

After the scripture readings, which are accompanied by numerous signs of the cross and acts of reverence, comes the sermon.

The sermon, which had almost completely disappeared from the Mass in the early Middle Ages, was revived by the mendicant preaching orders. Since it was the only part of the Mass in the vernacular (the language of the people; the rest of the Mass was in Latin), the sermon constituted a point of intersection with the faithful, who to this point had been following the Mass with a personal missal, when permitted, or praying privately. At various times and in various locations, the sermon became a focal point of the liturgy. The pulpit was often located in the middle of the nave of the church, so that people could hear better, given the absence of electronic sound amplification. It was fairly common for the priest to take off the chasuble, the outer colorful vestment, to give the sermon. This disrobing gave the impression that the sermon was not an essential part of the liturgy, rather, something of a time-out. For this reason the sermon did not necessarily reflect the readings of the day, but took on the air of a morality talk.

THE OFFERTORY

The second part of the Mass, called the offertory, reflected the eucharistic theology so prevalent since the Middle Ages ("Eucharist" means to give thanks. It refers to the part of worship that Protestants call "Communion" or "the Lord's Supper").

Unveiling the chalice and paten, the priest raises the elements of bread and wine and recites individual prayers that underscore the action of a propitiatory offering for sins. (Propitiate means "appease," as in appeasing God.) According to liturgical custom, it was a serious sin for one to be late for Mass, but the sin was considered mortal if the chalice and paten were already uncovered when the latecomer arrived.

A prayer to the most holy Trinity to bless and receive the offerings of the entire church follows. Then, turning to the people, the priest invites them to pray that his sacrifice and theirs may find acceptance with God. Turning back toward the altar, the priest next prays quietly. These prayers are called "the secrets" because they are said silently. These prayers lead to the preface concluded by the angelic hymn, "Holy, Holy, Holy." The structure of the beginning dialogue between priest and servers is a good indication of the dialogic nature of the Roman liturgy, although the people participate only vicariously, through the responses of the servers. The role of the priest and people is twofold: they offer themselves with Christ, the eternal victim, and with the preface, they herald the great sacrificial action itself.

THE CANON

The canon is the third part of the liturgy, referring to the consecratory prayer of blessing, which contains the account of the Last Supper. The eucharistic prayer summoned the church to join the angels and saints in thanking God, in proclaiming God's holiness, and in imploring God's help for the church. Because this prayer was said quietly, with many complicated and obscure gestures, the people participated as passive spectators only. For example, the celebrant looks up to the cross, extends and lifts his hands, then looks down while joining his hands. Next he bows, laying his hands on the altar, and begins the eucharistic prayer silently. Clearly, we are in the presence of high drama. Every stage direction is spelled out in great detail by the rubrics of the missal. Three signings of the cross with the right hand over the chalice and paten accompany the words "bless these † offerings, these † oblations, these † holy, unblemished sacrificial gifts," indicated by red crosses in the text.

The priest then bows while remembering those for whom he prays during the liturgy. The priest, united in fellowship with the Blessed Virgin, the holy apostles, martyrs, and all the saints becomes one with Christ who at the Last Supper commanded this action, "Do this in memory of me."

Spreading his hands over the elements in an action usually associated with summoning the Holy Spirit, he prays that the bread and wine might become a peace offering. This action is signaled by the ringing of the bells by the server.

Three more signs of the cross accompany the consecratory prayer "to make this offering wholly † blessed, a thing † consecrated and † approved." Then he makes the sign of the cross over the bread as he says "body" and another over the wine as he says "blood."

Taking the bread into his hands, he enters into the institutional narrative (see Matt 26:26), recalling the actions of Christ at the Last Supper. Every gesture is carefully detailed by the missal. As he says the words "lifting his eyes toward heaven," he looks up to the cross positioned high above the altar and then looks down again at once. "Giving thanks," he bows, and at the word "blessed" he again makes the sign of the cross over the host held in his left hand. Continuing, he says in a low voice while looking at the host, "For this is my body." As soon as he finishes saying these words, without delay, he stands erect and then genuflects on the right knee and elevates the host over his head for all present to see.

Similarly with the wine, he takes the chalice into his hands and bows over it, quietly recites the words of institution, once again blessing the cup at the appropriate cue, and elevates the cup over his head for all to see. The attitude of the priest and the assembled people is one of adoration, uniting their lives to the life of Christ. Although the complexity of the liturgical gesture is not fully visible to the assembled people, they are aware that this action is to be reenacted in memory of Christ.

To help the congregation in their devotional response, bells, either those in the church tower or hand bells rung by a server, signal the solemnity of the moment.

Once again, a triple sign of the cross accompanies the blessing of the sacrifice that is "pure †, holy †, and unblemished †" as well as two more signs of the cross, one over the "sacred Bread of everlasting life" and the other over "the Cup of eternal salvation."

Next he bows low over the altar and prays as a humble servant before Almighty God, kissing the altar when he speaks about the sacrifice. More signs of the cross are made over the eucharistic elements that accompany the words "body" and "blood," and the priest signs himself at the words "every grace and heavenly blessings."

When the priest prays for "thy sinful servants," he strikes his breast, while recalling a list of saints in whose company he seeks to be admitted, provided that his sins are forgiven.

As one might gather, the choreography of the liturgical prayer was terribly complicated, demanding the careful attention of the priest. In the short span of the eucharistic prayer, one can sense the redundancy of the liturgical gestures with the multiple signs of the cross, genuflections, and bows. Yet all these gestures were stringently governed by the rubrics in the missal, giving hardly any room for personal expression and devotion. Furthermore, since the priest had his back to the people, almost all of the liturgical gestures were totally obscured form the view of the worshiping assembly.

COMMUNION

The Our Father begins the preparation for Communion. During the Middle Ages, the reception of Communion was often limited to the priest. Given the strong penitential piety of the age, most people felt unworthy to receive the body and blood of the Lord. This sense of spiritual awe and personal unworthiness led to the practice of "ocular Communion" (gazing upon the consecrated host, the bread), an act of devotion. There are stories about people who would rush from church to church to see the elevation of the eucharistic elements and immediately depart as though they had seen the devil. Because the priest had his back to the people, blocking their view, people would cry out to him to lift the host higher so that they could see. There are other stories that people would drill holes into certain English churches so that they could peek in at the elevation. These contributed to the widespread practice of composing special musical pieces for the elevation. One consequence of this eucharistic piety was manifested in adoration of the host in special vessels called "monstrances." To combat many of these liturgical abuses and to encourage more frequent Communion by the faithful, the Fourth Lateran Council (1215 CE) required that all people receive the Eucharist at least once a year during the Easter season.

CONCLUSION

The high-drama Mass of the medieval era continued essentially unchanged in the Roman Catholic Church until the twentieth century.

In 1963 *The Constitution on the Sacred Liturgy* was published by the proceedings of the Catholic Council known as Vatican II. This constitution drastically changed the Roman liturgy, making it a liturgy of the people rather than a liturgy of the clergy.

While the contemporary Roman Catholic liturgy retains a sense of theater, the shift of Vatican II has moved the liturgy toward the recovery of intimacy. Now the Mass is in the language of the people, and the people truly participate in the drama.

The description of the Roman Mass is from Michael S. Driscoll, "The Roman Mass," in *Twenty Centuries of Christian Worship* (Hendrickson, 1994), pp. 171–86.

STUDY GUIDE

Read Session 5, "Dramatizing the Faith in Worship"
before starting the study guide.

PART I: PERSONAL STUDY

Complete the following questions individually.

1. *Life Connection*

*   It will be very difficult for most students of this course to make a life connection with the medieval Mass. This is so because in 1965 the Roman church changed the Mass significantly, putting it into the language of the people and to some extent making the Mass less dramatic. Nevertheless, enough of the Roman Mass remains to get a sense of its drama. So, if you are able, attend a Roman Mass. Or, research Roman Mass at the library and find a picture book that will help you visualize the drama. If you are not able to do either of the above, recall a Mass or portion of a Mass you have seen on television or remember a Mass you may have attended at a Catholic funeral or wedding. Write your impressions below.

    _____

    _____

    _____

    _____

    _____

2. *Content Questions*

*   Reread pp. "The Mass of the Catechumens," and list every dramatic action done by the priest. _____

    _____

    _____

    _____

    _____

◆ Reread "The Offertory" and list every dramatic action done by the priest.

_____

_____

_____

◆ Reread "The Canon" and list every dramatic action done by the priest.

_____

_____

_____

_____

◆ Reread "Communion" and list every dramatic action done by the priest.

_____

_____

_____

_____

PART II: GROUP DISCUSSION

The following questions are designed for group discussion.

1. *Life Connection*

◆ Begin your discussion by asking various members of the group to respond to the Catholic Mass either out of their experience of attending Mass or out of their study of it. Ask, "How did you experience the Mass as a drama?"

2. *Thought Questions*

◆ Give examples of worship experiences you have had that were intimate. How do they differ from services that are less intimate and more like a drama?

◆ Compare Acts 2:42–47 with Rev 4–5. List the evidences of intimacy mentioned in Acts 2:42–47 on the board. List the evidences of theater in Rev 4–5 on the board. Does God approve of both intimate worship and theatrical worship?

+ Drawing on the exercises you completed in Part I, review the dramatic elements of medieval Roman Catholic worship. Go through the following sections of the Mass one by one and write on the board all the elements of drama that you find in the description of medieval worship:

    The Mass of the catechumens
    The offertory
    The canon
    The Communion

+ Should our worship be a drama of the work of Christ?

3. *Application*

+ Does the worship of your church stress worship as a dramatic reenactment of the work of Christ or as an intimate relationship?

+ Is it possible for worship to be both intimate and theatrical (dramatic) at the same time? Explain.

+ Does the worship of your church need to be more intimate or more dramatic? Why? What improvement would you make?

REDISCOVERING THE WORD
A Study in Reformation Worship

I grew up in Montgomeryville, Pennsylvania, where my father was the pastor of a Baptist church. Like most other teenagers, I was aware of other Protestant traditions, but I didn't think much about them. I was simply prejudiced.

I assumed that I could learn nothing from these traditions because my tradition was in sole possession of the truth. In college I began to sort out the Protestant traditions as I learned about the history of Western civilization. It was at this time that the Reformation as an event of the sixteenth century first registered.

But I did not begin to explore the riches of the Reformation until I became a seminary student. I knew that the mainline Protestant traditions, such as the Lutherans, the various Calvinistic bodies, the Anglicans, and the Anabaptists, all originated in the sixteenth century, but that was about all I knew.

In seminary we studied the Reformation. We examined why the Reformers sought to change the Roman Church, how they broke with the Roman Church, and how they began a new movement in the Christian church that we have called the Protestant movement (from the word "protest").

For the most part, we studied the Reformation as a reform of doctrine. Certainly Luther and Calvin, as well as the Anabaptists and the Anglicans, were deeply concerned about doctrine. But an important point was overlooked in my education: The Reformation introduced vast changes in worship, as well as in doctrine.

WHY THE REFORMATION OF WORSHIP?

The early church taught that "the rule of prayer is the rule of faith." The saying means that worship shapes the way we believe.

The early church understood the power of worship to shape the beliefs of the worshiping community. The Reformers also understood this principle. And they knew that their doctrinal changes would only stick if they changed the worship of the people.

The Reformers were alarmed by the worship of the Roman Catholic Church in the fifteenth and early sixteenth centuries because they felt this worship taught the wrong doctrine. Two major concerns that all the Reformers expressed about Catholic worship were (1) the sacrificial nature of the Mass and (2) the doctrine of transubstantiation.

First, Protestants rejected the Mass because of the medieval view of it as a repetition of the sacrifice of Christ. Luther's most direct criticisms were aimed at the Roman prayers of the eucharistic canon. The Mass, Luther charged, had lost its original focus as a thanksgiving and had become a propitiation to please God. For Luther, this notion was incompatible with the Scriptures. It stood against the gospel and therefore had to be excised from worship. Furthermore, the theology of sacrifice in the Mass created numerous other problems. People expected to gain all sorts of benefits and advantages from hearing Mass, including healings, the release of souls from purgatory, and other magical results. The Mass had even lost the idea of Communion because people did not have to be present at the Mass—it could be said on their behalf. Consequently, the priest saying the Mass replaced worship by the people and became a legalistic means of buying salvation. This understanding struck at the heart of the Christian message and perverted the essential nature of the Christian faith as a religion of grace. The Mass as a sacrifice had to be rejected. In this all the Protestants concurred.

Second, the Reformers rejected the doctrine of transubstantiation (the belief that the bread and wine became the actual body of Christ). The substance of bread and wine changed into the body and blood of Christ and was offered to the Father as a sacrifice for salvation. The connection between the Mass as a sacrifice and the doctrine of transubstantiation naturally led the Reformers, who rejected the one, to reject the other as well.

THE GOAL OF REFORMATION WORSHIP

Today any number of Christian leaders voice the opinion that we must "go back to the early church." Renewal movements throughout the ages have wanted to recapture the emphasis and fervor of the early church.

The Reformers were no exception to this rule.

A major change that all the Reformers wanted to make in worship was to restore the preaching of the Word. In the Roman tradition the preaching of the Word had lost its place of importance in worship. Some priests might deliver a homily dealing with moral matters, but the teaching and preaching of Scripture had largely disappeared.

A second change desired by all the Reformers was to restore worship to the language of the people. The Roman liturgy had, of course, developed in the Roman world when Latin was the language of the people. But as the Roman Church spread among the Germans, the French, the Swiss, and the English, it did not adapt to the language of the people. Some converts learned Latin, but most did not. The Reformers wanted to return worship to the people, so one of their first acts was to translate worship into a language that they could understand.

In addition to restoring scripture-reading, preaching, and worship in the language of the people, the Reformers wanted to restore the ancient structure of worship that included both preaching the Word and celebrating the Eucharist (the Lord's Supper). They knew that the early church proclaimed, enacted, and celebrated the living, dying, and rising of Christ. And they wanted to do the same. Unfortunately, their emphasis on preaching the Word was so strong and the association of the Eucharist with Roman Catholic worship so fixed in people's minds that a balance between Word and Sacrament was not achieved.

In the twentieth century the worship renewal movement is striving to recover both preaching and Communion as essential to worship. The Roman Catholic Church is recovering the place of the sermon, and many Protestant churches are restoring the Lord's Supper to its rightful place.

DIFFERENCES AMONG THE REFORMATION CHURCHES

The Reformers were united in their opposition to Catholic worship, in their desire to restore the Word, to return worship to the people, and to recover the balance of Word and sacrament. But the various Reformers proposed very different styles of worship. The Lutheran and Anglican traditions retained much of ancient worship; the Zwinglians and the Anabaptists made a radical break with the past; and the Reformed church maintained a middle position.

Lutheran and Anglican worship retains a good bit of ceremony but is quite simple when compared with medieval worship. The most drastic approach was taken by Zwingli and the Anabaptists. Zwingli repudiated all ceremonies as pagan and commenced to rid the church of traditions and worship rubrics, regardless of their possible value to the church. He was convinced that faith came through the Holy Spirit without any physical channels or external means.

The Anabaptists rejected not only ceremonies in worship but also the necessity of formal public worship. They defined the true church as an obedient and suffering people whose daily walk with God was of utmost importance. This walk climaxed in the gathering of Christians together for prayer, Bible reading, admonition, and the Lord's Supper in the informal atmosphere of the home. They refused to attend the worship of the state church and met in secret at various times in an unscheduled and impromptu manner. The time and place of their meetings were communicated by word of mouth to those who belonged to the closely knit community.

The Reformed community forged out a mediating approach to worship. Their worship is much less ceremonial than that of Luther or the Anglicans. On the other hand, it is more complex than that of the Anabaptists and the Protestant tradition in general.

CONCLUSION

Protestant Christianity and Protestant worship originated in the sixteenth century. The changes instituted by the Reformers represented an attempt to get back to an earlier form of worship. But differences of opinion existed about how extensively worship should be purified. Should the worship of the church be based on the teaching of the Bible alone? Or, is it appropriate to retain some ceremonial elements? These were vital questions that we are still asking today.

Portions of this chapter were taken from Robert E. Webber, *Worship Old and New* (Zondervan, 1982) pp. 73–78. For a more detailed study of Reformation worship see *Twenty Centuries of Christian Worship* (Hendrickson, 1994), pp. 188–226.

STUDY GUIDE

Read Session 6, "Rediscovering the Word," before starting the study guide.

PART I: PERSONAL STUDY

Complete the following questions individually.

1. *Life Connection*

* This session looks at Reformation worship, a worship that has changed significantly since the sixteenth century. To enhance your understanding of this subject, attend a worship service that is Lutheran, Reformed, Anglican or Mennonite. If you cannot attend one of these services, try to recall a worship in one of these traditions from your past. Describe your impressions.

  _____

  _____

  _____

  _____

  _____

2. *Content Questions*

* What is the meaning of the phrase "the rule of prayer is the rule of faith"?

  _____

  _____

  _____

  _____

  _____

* What were the Reformers' main concerns regarding Roman worship?

  _____

  _____

  _____

  _____

- Why did Luther view the Mass as an abuse? _____
  _____
  _____
  _____
  _____
  _____

- What is the difference between the Mass as a propitiation and the Eucharist as a thanksgiving? _____
  _____
  _____
  _____
  _____
  _____

- Why did the Reformers reject the doctrine of transubstantiation?
  _____
  _____
  _____
  _____
  _____

- Why did the Reformers want to recapture the preaching of the Word?
  _____
  _____
  _____
  _____
  _____
  _____

- Why did the Reformers reject worship in Latin? _____
  _____
  _____
  _____
  _____
  _____

♦ Draw a graph that shows the attitudes of various Reformation traditions toward ancient worship.

♦ Why did Zwingli espouse a plain and simple approach to worship?

_____

_____

_____

_____

_____

_____

♦ Why did the Anabaptists reject public worship conducted in the state church?

_____

_____

_____

_____

_____

3. *Application*

♦ What views about worship have been handed down in the life of your church? State them below. _____

_____

_____

_____

_____

- If you are a Protestant, which of the Reformers, if any, have influenced your approach to worship? _____

_____

_____

_____

_____

PART II: GROUP QUESTIONS

The following questions are designed for group discussion.

1. *Life Connection*
- Begin by asking several members of the class to discuss their experience of worship in one or another of the Protestant traditions of worship. Try to obtain responses to Lutheran, Reformed, Anglican, and Anabaptist worship. Write the responses on the board. Compare them to get a feeling for how these Reformation churches differ from one another in their worship.

2. *Thought Questions*
- Calvin taught that worship should be guided by "only that which is explicitly taught in Scripture," while Luther taught that "in worship we are free to use whatever is not explicitly condemned in scripture." Thus Calvin's worship was simple and plain, while Luther's worship included more ceremonial and symbolic elements. Whom do you agree with and why? Put the answer on the board.
- How does the worship of your church shape what you believe?
- What is the attitude of your church toward Communion? Is it understood as a propitiation, a thanksgiving, or a memorial? Explain your answer.
- Is the central act of worship the reading and preaching of the Word or the celebration of Communion? How would the Reformers have answered this question?

- If Luther were to attend a worship service in your church, what would he want to change? Calvin? Zwingli? Cranmer (an Anglican)? Menno (a Mennonite)?

3. *Application*

- Today the worship of many churches is more eclectic than it was in the past. Examine every aspect of your present worship and ask, "What parts of the worship of this church have been shaped by Reformation worship?"

- Ask, "How would it be received if we asked a Lutheran, Reformed, Anglican, or Mennonite pastor to lead our church in a service of worship from his or her tradition?

IN SEARCH OF BIBLICAL WORSHIP

A Study in Protestant Free Church Worship, 1700–1900

Even though I grew up in the free church tradition of Christianity, I didn't understand what the term meant. Nor did I know how to distinguish the free church tradition from the ancient churches or from the Reformation churches.

I first learned about the distinction between these traditions when I went to seminary. I learned that the Eastern Orthodox Church and the Roman Catholic Church are called the "ancient liturgical churches." I learned that the churches of the Reformation—the Lutheran, Reformed and Anglican churches—are also referred to as "state churches" because they were the official churches of certain countries. For example, the Lutheran Church was the official church of Germany and the Anglican Church was the official church of England. These churches were also called "territorial" churches because no other church bodies were allowed to exist in their territory.

The idea of a "territorial church" seems strange to us today. In my own town of Wheaton there are more than fifty churches, each one bearing a different name. No one thinks anything of it. Two friends could walk to church, one going to a Lutheran church and the other going to a Reformed church. But accepting different traditions was not the case back in the early seventeenth century. There was only one church in a particular state, and everyone was expected to belong to that church.

But the human spirit, particularly the one growing in the late sixteenth and early seventeenth centuries, was far too independent to be constrained by a uniform experience for long. The earliest rejection of the state church concept was expressed in the sixteenth century by the Anabaptists (modern Hutterites, Amish, Mennonites, and Church of the Brethren). They argued against any alignment between church and state, emphasizing the church as a family of people that existed independently of the state. This was a radical idea for the sixteenth and seventeenth centuries. But the Anabaptists and others after them eventually won their independence from the state. Pluralism was born, and eventually towns contained the ancient liturgical churches, the state churches, and the free churches—all side by side. Free churches distinguished themselves not only in their independence from the state but also in their independence from tradition. They rejected most if not all of tradition and called for a church and a worship based on Scripture alone.

While each of these churches has its own unique style, there are three characteristics common to the free church movement: (1) the antiliturgical stance of all free churches; (2) the teaching approach to worship taken by seventeenth- and eighteenth-century churches; (3) the evangelistic approach to worship taken by churches of the nineteenth century.

THE ANTILITURGICAL STANCE OF THE FREE CHURCH MOVEMENT

One of the major characteristics of people in the free church movement is an aversion toward liturgy. Many contemporary free church worshipers prefer not to do the same thing in worship twice, have a disdain for high church order, and regard prayers that are read as evidence of a lack of personal spirituality.

These convictions lie deep within the soul of free church people. They issue from a spirituality that can be traced back to the founding of the free church movement in the seventeenth century. John Smyth, an early Baptist, insisted that worship should proceed only from the heart. For this reason he rejected the use of any book in worship. For example, the Bible could be read, but it would be wrong for the people to follow the reading with the Bible in hand. Hymnbooks were also forbidden. Singing consisted of "lining out the psalm." In this type of song, the leader would sing a psalm phrase by phrase, and the people sang responsively.

Congregationalists rejected the use of written prayers, insisting that prayer should be from the heart, directed by the Spirit of God. In support of this view they set forth six arguments: (1) written prayers deprive the person of his or her own thoughts and words; (2) set forms could not meet the variety of needs in a particular congregation; (3) set forms are idolatrous, as they equate the liturgy with the Bible; (4) set forms lead to overfamiliarity and lack of interest; (5) imposing set forms is a manner of persecution because each congregation should be "free" to follow its own desires; (6) set prayers oppose the appropriate approach to the Father.

Quaker worship is characterized by its abandoning the ordained ministry and the sacraments in favor of a personal "waiting upon the Spirit" by every member of the congregation. The central concern of Quaker worship is the simple intention of the people of God to open themselves to the presence of Christ in the meeting ("where two or three come together in my name, there am I with them") and to wait upon him to speak through the Spirit. This view rejects any dependence on external aids or rites such as the sacraments (in extreme groups the Spirit's revelation is more important than the Bible). It argues that all ceremonies and forms have been abolished by the new covenant and that the offices of Christ as prophet, priest, and king are exercised in the worshiping community as it silently waits upon him. Worship is supremely *inward*. Water baptism has been made unnecessary by Spirit baptism, and the Eucharist is an inward spiritual reception of Jesus that has no need of an external rite.

These ideas still prevail in many worshiping communities of the twentieth century. While a number of churches that were a part of the original free church movement are now adopting worship resources from the liturgical churches, many of the twentieth-century worship movements, such as the Pentecostals, the independent charismatic churches, and the praise and worship movement, retain many of the convictions of the free church movement.

The "Teaching" Approach to Worship Taken by the Seventeenth- and Eighteenth-Century Churches

Today we often distinguish between churches that emphasize the mind and churches that emphasize the heart. Most of us recognize this distinction as false since we are to love and worship God with all our heart and with all our mind. Nevertheless, we perpetuate this distinction because it is deeply rooted in the history of free church worship. For example, churches that were birthed in the seventeenth and eighteenth centuries tend to emphasize the mind and "knowing God," while churches of the nineteenth century tend to emphasize the heart and "experiencing God."

Puritan churches were strong on the "teaching" approach to worship. For example, here is a description of Puritan worship:

> At the Communion table, close to the worshiping congregation, the clergy often presided with lay leaders. Standing at the table with the people, clergy began the service with prayers of thanksgiving and later led prayers of intercession incorporating concerns spoken out or written by laity. All continued to stand for singing led by laity. Often from the table, clergy read the Scriptures interspersed with exegesis so that the Word would be heard truly and actively. Then the clergy went into the pulpit to give their sermons, applying the Bible to any of a wide range of issues related

to God's kingdom on earth. Immediately after the sermon, as worship continued, they came down from the pulpit and sat at the table to answer the congregation's questions and hear witnessing by laity who were free to agree or disagree with what was said in the sermon. From the table, clergy gave thanks and gave the bread and wine to lay leaders who distributed Communion to the people. After more singing, the people often gave their offerings at the table. Communion was celebrated as often as each Sunday or at least once a month. (Darrell Todd Maurina, "An American Puritan Model of Worship," in *Twenty Centuries of Christian Worship*, p. 227)

This description of worship and the setting in which it took place emphasizes worship as learning about God. The church was seen as a school, and worship was the classroom setting in which this learning took place. Although this approach to worship served those who participated in it well, it is not the only free church view of worship. There is also the worship of the heart, an emotional view of worship.

THE EVANGELISTIC APPROACH TO WORSHIP TAKEN BY THE CHURCHES OF THE NINETEENTH CENTURY

We are all familiar with evangelistic crusades and what is called revival worship. I grew up in a church that emphasized revival. Every spring our church had its annual revival week.

In the seventeenth and eighteenth centuries evangelistic crusades and revival meetings did not exist. Evangelistic crusades were introduced by John and Charles Wesley and were continued by Charles Finney, Billy Sunday, and Billy Graham. Revivalism, as we know it, began in the nineteenth century.

Fires of revival that broke out in the nineteenth century consumed the Puritan approach to worship just described, introducing a new order of worship and a new setting for worship. Both are still evident in many churches today.

What was new at the heart of worship was not so much learning about God as experiencing God. The goal of worship was conversion, not knowledge. The preacher's central concern was not so much the increase of knowledge, but the response of the heart.

This shift from head to heart resulted in significant changes in the order of worship and in the arrangement of the space in which worship took place.

Worship shifted from participation to presentation. The main drama of worship was now played out by the pastor, whose sermons not only proclaimed the Word of God but frequently acted it out through body and facial gestures. Worship itself shifted from the head to the heart. The entire order of worship was designed to move the sinner to repentance and faith. The main response of the people was to come forward to repent of sin and receive Christ by faith.

One can visualize the change in the order of worship through the change in the arrangement of space. Now everyone faced forward toward the preacher and the choir. The space took on the atmosphere of the "platform" and the "audience" as worship shifted toward the revivalistic emphasis. Even the placement and the size of the Communion table expressed this shift. Communion, once central to the worship of the church, was now replaced by the invitation. The pulpit was given a central place in space and the Communion table was significantly cut down in size and placed beneath the pulpit.

All those images reinforced the message: "You have come to hear the message of salvation proclaimed in song and sermon. What God wants from you is a repentant attitude and the response of faith." This is worship with a new twist. It is a proclaiming of the living, dying, and rising of Christ. But it is no longer an enactment, as in the ancient churches, and it is no longer a teaching having to do with the message, as in the Puritan churches. It is now proclamation worship, worship that is fulfilled by the heart's response to receive Jesus as Lord and Savior.

CONCLUSION

This session describes a world of worship experiences that is most familiar to Protestants. While revival worship is still practiced among many congregations in the free church tradition, many Reformation churches were widely influenced by this approach as well.

In the late twentieth century the revival approach to worship is being replaced in many churches by the praise and worship style of worship. We will learn more about that in Session 12.

Portions of this chapter were adapted from Robert E. Webber, *Worship Old and New* (Zondervan, 1982), pp. 79–84. For further information on free church worship, see chapter 10, "Post-Reformation Models of Worship" in *Twenty Centuries of Christian Worship*, pp. 227–58.

STUDY GUIDE

Read Session 7, "In Search of Biblical Worship,"
before starting the study guide.

PART I: PERSONAL STUDY

Complete the following questions individually.

1. *Life Connection*

◆ If you have never attended a free church worship try to do so. Free church worship ranges from Baptist to Quaker churches. Some Baptist churches are more formal than others. Other options include Congregational, Evangelical Free, and many independent evangelical churches. If you cannot attend a worship, you may want to stop by a church of the free tradition and ask for a bulletin. Then describe your impression of free church worship.

_____

_____

_____

_____

_____

_____

_____

2. *Content Questions*

◆ How does a free church differ from a state or territorial church?

_____

_____

_____

_____

_____

_____

◆ Why did the Anabaptists argue against the state church?_____

_____

_____

_____

_____

◆ What are the characteristics of the free church movement?

_____

_____

_____

_____

_____

◆ Why do free church worshipers have an aversion to liturgy? _____

_____

_____

_____

_____

_____

◆ Summarize in your own words the convictions of John Smyth, an early
Baptist._____

_____

_____

_____

_____

◆ In your own words summarize the six arguments against written prayers,
as set forth by the Congregationalists. _____

_____

_____

_____

_____

◆ Summarize in your own words the arguments for simplicity of worship, as set forth by the Quakers. _____

_____

_____

_____

_____

_____

◆ What was the central idea of free church worship in the seventeenth and eighteenth centuries? _____

_____

_____

_____

_____

_____

◆ Study the description of Puritan worship, then set down the order of worship in your own words._____

_____

_____

_____

_____

_____

◆ What new emphasis in worship was introduced by the nineteenth-century revivalists? _____

_____

_____

_____

_____

◆ Draw a picture of the worship space in a presentational worship church.

3. *Application*

◆ Does your church reflect one or more of the three characteristics of the free church movement? Explain. _____

_____

_____

_____

_____

◆ Does your church differ from one or more of the three characteristics of the free church movement? Explain. _____

_____

_____

_____

_____

PART II: GROUP DISCUSSION

The following questions are designed for group discussion.

1. *Life Connection*

◆ Begin your discussion by asking several group members to comment on their experience in the free church movement. What differences do they find in the worship of various free churches? How do they account for these differences? How do they feel about free church worship?

2. *Thought Questions*

- Do you think it is better for the church to allow freedom of worship styles or should there be one state church? Why?

- What do you think of the arguments against written prayers set forth by the Congregationalists?

- Do you think Quaker worship goes too far in its rejection of liturgy? Why? Do you think its worship is the logical conclusion of the argument for free church worship?

- Contrast the "mind-centered" worship of the seventeenth and eighteenth centuries with the "heart-centered" worship of the nineteenth century. Which worship would you prefer and why?

- Do you think worship should be ordered or do you think worship should be an open, spontaneous work of the people?

- Do you think worship should be a program of various worship acts or a narrative rehearsing God's work of salvation and our response? Why?

3. *Application*

- In what way is the worship of your church like the worship of the free church tradition. In what ways is it different? Put your answers on the board.

- What can your church learn and incorporate from the free church tradition? What can the free church tradition of worship learn from your worship? Put your answers on the board.

- Do you think that a convergence of historic and contemporary approaches to worship is possible? What would such a worship look like?

CONVERSIONS

The life of a slave was unnaturally constricted and was characterized by anxiety and tension. Relief from anxiety, moral cleansing, and regeneration could take place through the experience of worship and through conversion (for some). Personal status and affirmation could be realized through visions, dreams, and imagination, which convinced individuals of their worth. A "knock-down" conversion experience unleashed these forms of behavior. Conversion imparted to the slaves the awareness that God had already freed them to walk in God's glory. Since for some the state of "not knowing" (not having had a personal encounter) was sinful, the convert would identify his or her experience as a release from sin. Shouting was often linked with emotional conversion experiences, as evidence of the fire of the "Holy Ghost" burning inside. Shouting was an evidence of conversion—an outward demonstration of the inner joy that came from an encounter with the divine.

TESTIMONIES

If time permitted, the people offered personal testimonies in worship, an act that made a definite impact on the corporate community. All could claim the experiences and learn from them, so that they were enabled to walk together in the testimonies of others.

CLOSING

There is little evidence of an exact form for closing worship; there was singing and sometimes a prayer. Because the meetings were clandestine it may have been necessary to end them abruptly if an outsider happened to approach. Prayers and songs attest to words of parting that served as a benediction:

Lord, make me more holy . . .
    Until we meet again.
Lord, make me more faithful . . .
    Until we meet again.
Lord, make me more loving . . .
    Until we meet again.

CONCLUSION

All Christians can learn a great deal from African-American worship. It is a worship that was born out of considerable pain and sorrow; it is a worship characterized by a considerable amount of freedom; it is a worship that engages the whole person, not merely the mind. In this worship people were healed and made to feel part of the community of God's people. It is a wonderful experience of being relocated in God.

Interestingly, many of the worship songs that are gaining popularity today, as well as the entire praise and worship movement, bear a kinship to African-American worship.

Most of the content of this chapter was either adapted or taken in whole from Melva Costen, "African American Worship," in *Twenty Centuries of Christian Worship*, pp. 249–51.

STUDY GUIDE

Read Session 8, "Soul Worship," before starting the study guide.

PART I: PERSONAL STUDY

Complete the following questions individually.

1. *Life Connection*
- Nearly all American Christians have attended an African-American worship or at least watched one on television. If you have not done so, make a special effort to attend or to watch a service before completing this lesson. Record your impressions below. How does African-American worship differ from your worship? In what ways is it similar? _____

  _____

  _____

  _____

  _____

  _____

  _____

2. *Content Questions*
- Why did the slaves find their masters' forms of worship to be oppressive?

  _____

  _____

  _____

  _____

  _____

- How did the slaves cope with the slaveholders' restrictions? _____

  _____

  _____

  _____

  _____

- What kind of message did the slaves hear in their clandestine worship?

  _____
  _____
  _____
  _____
  _____

- Euro-American preaching is usually given to reason and logic, which many people find dull. Describe African-American preaching. _____

  _____
  _____
  _____
  _____

- Outline the order of clandestine worship. _____

  _____
  _____
  _____
  _____

- How does the order of worship that you just described differ from the order of worship in your church? _____

  _____
  _____
  _____
  _____
  _____
  _____

- What strikes you as unusual or unique about the call to worship? _____

  _____
  _____
  _____
  _____

● In your own words describe the feelings that the slaves must have felt in the gathering. _____

_____

_____

_____

_____

● Why do you think there is such "soul" to African-American singing?

_____

_____

_____

_____

● What words describe the emotion of prayer? _____

_____

_____

_____

_____

● What words describe the heart of preaching? _____

_____

_____

_____

_____

● Why did shouting occur in clandestine worship? _____

_____

_____

_____

_____

● Describe the experience of conversion for a slave. _____

_____

_____

_____

- What was the importance of testimonies in slave worship?_____

_____

_____

_____

_____

_____

- What kind of feelings do you think slaves experienced as they parted
  from worship? _____

_____

_____

_____

_____

_____

_____

3. *Application*

- Think back through the lesson you have read and the questions you
  have answered. Why do you suppose slave worship and African-American worship today is so full of soul, while much Euro-American worship
  is lacking in feeling? _____

_____

_____

_____

_____

_____

PART II: GROUP DISCUSSION

The following questions are designed for group discussion.

1. *Life Connection*

- Begin your group discussion by asking various members of the group to
  describe their experiences in African-American worship. What makes
  this style of worship so appealing?

2. *Thought Questions*

- Worship often takes on added meaning when we are going through a difficult time. When we experience a life-threatening situation like an operation or an incurable disease, or when death or divorce has occurred in the family, we often feel a strong need to worship. The reason for this is that worship touches us in our dislocations and relocates us in God. Discuss this idea and ask if anyone in the group has experienced this. Now ask, "Do you think Euro-American worship lacks soul because whites never experienced the kind of dislocations experienced by blacks? Or do you think this lack of feeling stems from other reasons?"

- Holiness, Pentecostal, and charismatic worship, as well as contemporary praise and worship style, has more "soul" than mainline Protestant or evangelical worship. Why is this so?

- Why do you think African-American worship is more participatory than Euro-American worship?

- Do you prefer participatory or nonparticipatory worship? Why?

- African-American preaching is colorful and given to storytelling. What reason can you suggest for this?

- Do you prefer explanatory preaching or more imaginative, narrative preaching? Why?

3. *Application*

- What aspects of African-American worship would you like to see incorporated into the worship of your church? List them on the board and explain.

- Prepare a prayer in African-American style.

- Read the story of the prodigal son (Luke 15:11–32). How would this story be developed in an African-American style of preaching?

PART III

∽∿∾

WORSHIP

RENEWAL IN

THE TWENTIETH

CENTURY

TONGUES OF FIRE

A Study in Pentecostal Worship

 I have already mentioned that I was raised in the free church tradition. Today that tradition is usually referred to as "evangelical."

Within the evangelical tradition there are at least two streams of churches that are very different in theological orientation and worship style. One of these streams has been influenced by the teachings of John Calvin; the other has been influenced by the writings and the work of John Wesley.

For example, most independent Bible churches, as well as conservative denominations such as the Evangelical Free Church, the Conservative Baptist churches, and the Baptist General Conference are at least loosely associated with John Calvin. They do not affirm all of Calvin's theology, but generally they are in that stream of thought.

On the other hand, many churches of the holiness movement, such as the Wesleyan Church, the Nazarene Church, the Christian and Missionary Alliance Church, and the Pentecostal churches, such as the Assemblies of God churches or the Church of God in Christ, are churches that have been influenced by a particular stream of thought traceable to John Wesley. The specific side of Wesley that these churches stress is a second work of grace or what is also called the baptism of the Holy Spirit. This work of God's grace is evidenced in worship through the recovery of the gift of tongues, which is regarded as a fulfillment of Peter's Pentecost sermon (Acts 2:17–21; tongues being a particular emphasis of Pentecostals not found among the holiness groups) and in a worship that is significantly more expressive and enthusiastic than the Calvinistic side of evangelicalism.

In this study we will trace the origins and the worship style of the holiness churches and the Pentecostal churches. Both of these worshiping communities have been shaped by the enthusiasm of John Wesley. We draw upon the work of a Pentecostal scholar, Edith Blumhofer.

THE HOLINESS BACKGROUND

The American holiness movement traces its origins to John Wesley and his associate, John Fletcher, who were persuaded that a conversion experience should always be followed by a dynamic encounter with sanctifying grace. In the nineteenth century people from many denominations gathered in camp meetings and brush arbors around the country for simple teaching, enthusiastic singing, and agonizing prayer. The most radical among them gradually severed their relationships with historic denominations. Over several decades they generated a new cluster of holiness denominations such as the Church of the Nazarene, the Free Methodist Church, and the Wesleyan Church.

THE DESIRE FOR INTENSE RELIGIOUS EXPERIENCE

Methodists were well-known for pursuing intense religious experiences and for "raising the shout" when they "broke through" and experienced grace. They sang the majestic hymns that Charles Wesley had bequeathed to them, the pietist hymns that John Wesley translated from German, and the simple songs of exhortation and testimony that came out of revivals and camp meetings. Because they dealt in truths that touched the deepest human emotions, they regarded tears, groans, vocal praise, and audible individual prayer as appropriate, even necessary, in corporate and individual worship. They made room in their services for personal testimonies, partly because testifying to an experience seemed to them to be part of "owning" or appropriating that experience for themselves.

THE HOLINESS EXPERIENCE OF WORSHIP

Holiness emphases on grace and cleansing generated a holiness idiom that found expression in devotional literature and gospel songs. The new style used Old Testament stories of Israel's crossing the Jordan into Canaan as analogies for the "second definite work of grace" and the "baptism with the Holy Spirit." Like early Methodism, it emphasized the blood of Jesus. It popularized the holiness experience as both an end and a beginning: it ended the first phase of the Christian life and introduced believers into a new dimension of Christian living. It made them "happy" and "free" and gave them assurance of cleansing from sin. A significant number of the gospel songs that were incorporated into the hymnals of twentieth-century evangelicals express the sentiments of these women and men whose deep religious experiences seemed to find musical expression naturally.

One wing of the holiness movement, the Salvation Army, was often denounced for setting religious words to popular secular tunes. The Salvation Army also popularized the use of band instruments in outdoor evangelism and worship services. Parading through city streets in military-style uniforms and playing popular melodies, they regularly drew crowds that responded to their vernacular style.

Holiness people gathered in all kinds of settings, formal and informal: camp meetings, brush arbors, tabernacles, missions, homes, churches. They welcomed participation by everyone in attendance, often providing opportunities for both corporate and individual involvement as well as structured and spontaneous participation. The movement made a rich contribution to American religion, not least through the thousands of songs written to express the admittedly inexpressible bliss of the sanctified soul.

THE EMERGENCE OF THE PENTECOSTAL MOVEMENT

After 1901, Pentecostalism emerged as an identifiable religious movement. It appropriated much of the idiom of the holiness movement, reinterpreting some of it to nuance its understanding of the baptism with the Holy Spirit. Many of the songs Pentecostals have sung over the years to describe their experiences were written before the emergence of Pentecostalism, by holiness people intent on describing sanctifying grace. The two movements shared religious language about life in the Spirit that nevertheless carried very different theological connotations in the two movements.

ORIGINAL PENTECOSTAL WORSHIP

A unique feature of Pentecostal worship is known as "singing in the Spirit." This involves one, several, or all the gathered worshipers in singing simultaneously and harmoniously, either in tongues or in the vernacular. As a congregation sings a song of worship, individual songs of praise begin to be heard. Singing in the same key and moving among several basic chords, individuals express their feelings in words that are meaningful to them. The music may seem to flow from one individual to another, the voice of one occasioning another's participation until many are involved. Participants believe that the Holy Spirit orchestrates all of the worshipers. Sometimes individuals who are understood by those around them to be "in the Spirit" may sing solos that hearers describe as beautiful songs.

Aimee Semple McPherson, one of the most prolific Pentecostal musicians, used innovative worship techniques that extensively influenced American Pentecostalism. Reared in the Salvation Army but converted to Pentecostalism by an evangelist she later married, McPherson blended the holiness and Pentecostal traditions with such creativity that she came to be hailed as Los Angeles' premier star in the 1920s. Her dramatic entry into her pulpit at the 5,000-seat Angelus Temple was always preceded by thirty minutes of singing led by award-winning choirs and accompanied by an excellent orchestra seated in a hydraulically-operated orchestra pit. She composed songs for her people, operas for their holiday entertainment, and graphic sermons to convey her message. She represented a style that gained increasing favor among Pentecostals, a style that featured one or more performing stars. She altered the nature of individual participation, which she professed to value but at the same time insisted on controlling. In many ways her style was the trend of the future.

CONTEMPORARY HOLINESS AND PENTECOSTAL WORSHIP

In recent years, the holiness and Pentecostal movements have significantly modified the form and content of their worship. Some denominations have become more like other evangelicals in both their music and their worship style. On the other hand, the charismatic renewal has generated a fresh musical style that has greatly influenced Pentecostalism. Rejecting much of the traditional hymnody and the gospel songs of an earlier era as outdated, charismatics opt for simple choruses. They set Scripture to music or compose worship choruses that enable people to express their feelings, their experiences, and their praise. In many Pentecostal congregations, overhead transparencies have virtually replaced hymnals, which are used selectively if at all.

CONCLUSION

This brief survey of Pentecostal worship demonstrates that it is in many ways a forerunner of the modern praise and worship movement, which emphasizes informality and spontaneity.

Most of the material of this session was adapted from Edith Blumhofer, "The Holiness-Pentecostal Movement," in *Twenty Centuries of Christian Worship*, pp. 105–8.

STUDY GUIDE

Read Session 9, "Tongues of Fire," before starting the study guide.

PART I: PERSONAL STUDY

Complete the following questions individually.

1. *Life Connection*
- Pentecostal Christianity is one of the fastest-growing expressions of the faith in the world, and some members of your group have probably attended or at least visited a Pentecostal church. If you have not worshiped in a Pentecostal setting by all means attempt to do so. Describe your impressions of Pentecostal worship. _____

_____

_____

_____

2. *Content Questions*
- What churches are generally affected by the thought of the sixteenth-century Reformer, John Calvin? _____

_____

_____

_____

_____

- What churches are generally affected by the thought of the eighteenth-century revivalist, John Wesley? _____

_____

_____

_____

_____

- What teaching is common to the churches influenced by John Wesley?
  _____
  _____
  _____
  _____

- How do Wesleyan groups differ from Calvinist groups? _____
  _____
  _____
  _____
  _____

- What stands at the core of the American holiness movement? _____
  _____
  _____
  _____
  _____

- Where did this movement originate? _____
  _____
  _____
  _____
  _____

- How can the experience of the "second definite work of grace" or the "baptism of the Holy Spirit" be described? _____
  _____
  _____
  _____
  _____

- Why was the Salvation Army denounced by some? _____
  _____
  _____
  _____
  _____

◆ What controversy raged within the holiness movement? _____

_____

_____

_____

_____

◆ Describe Pentecostal worship._____

_____

_____

_____

_____

◆ Singing has always been central to Pentecostal worship. What do Pentecostals accomplish in their singing? _____

_____

_____

_____

_____

◆ What is "singing in the Spirit"? _____

_____

_____

_____

_____

◆ How did Aimee Semple McPherson alter Pentecostal worship? _____

_____

_____

_____

_____

◆ How have holiness and Pentecostal worship changed in the twentieth
century? _____

_____

_____

_____

3. *Application*

• What elements of Pentecostal worship would you like to see incorporated into the worship of your church? _____

_____

_____

_____

_____

_____

PART II: GROUP DISCUSSION

The following questions are designed for group discussion.

1. *Life Connection*

• Begin your discussion by asking several members of the group to tell about their experience with a holiness or Pentecostal worship.

2. *Thought Questions*

• What are the similarities between African-American worship (Session 8) and holiness-Pentecostal worship. Write your answers on the board.

• How does holiness-Pentecostal worship differ from the worship of mainline or evangelical churches? Write your answers on the board.

• Why is it that some people are attracted to more emotional worship while others are attracted to a worship that is more intellectual? Write your answers on the board.

• Read 1 Cor 12. What is the place of tongues in worship?

• Do you think that the changes that have occurred in holiness-Pentecostal worship in the twentieth century exert a positive or negative effect? Why?

• The charismatic renewal has significantly influenced the holiness-Pentecostal style of worship. Do you regard this influence as positive or negative?

3. *Application*

- What element(s) of holiness-Pentecostal worship would you like to see incorporated into the worship of your church?

- Write a description of the order of your worship on the board. Brainstorm on what elements of holiness-Pentecostal worship would work best for you.

DO ALL IN DECENCY AND IN ORDER

A Study in Contemporary Liturgical Renewal

 In 1964 I was living in Chattanooga, Tennessee, where I was teaching theology at Covenant College. I heard about recent worship changes in Roman Catholic worship that resulted from the promulgation of the *Constitution on the Sacred Liturgy*. The person who told me about the liturgical revolution was so enthusiastic that I decided to visit a Catholic church in the city.

I had studied the Church and its liturgy. I knew that the Mass was said in Latin and that the people, for the most part, watched and listened as the clergy did the liturgy.

I was in for quite a shock (as I'm sure the Catholic worshipers were also) when I attended this worship. First of all, the liturgy was now said in the language of the people. The order of worship and the prayers of the liturgy had been changed, and the reading and preaching of Scripture held a new place of prominence. Hymns and songs had been introduced (we sang Martin Luther's hymn, "A Mighty Fortress is Our God") and the atmosphere of worship had become considerably more casual.

In short, worship was in the process of being returned to the people. While not all people were happy about this (many to this day are still not pleased), the church indeed intended that worship be done by the people.

The revolution in the Catholic Church was soon felt in Protestant circles as well. Mainline Protestant churches had paid very little attention to their worship since the Reformation. Slight changes had been introduced through the years, and new Protestant movements had developed new styles of worship (e.g., free church movements, holiness-Pentecostals). But for the most part churches that traced their roots to the Reformation had never undergone any real revolution in their worship.

As Protestants studied reforms in Catholic worship, they came to look at their own worship. Eventually every mainline church has produced new resources for worship that reflect the influences of the Catholic reforms.

All these churches now face the task of bringing life to the worship of the local church. Renewal in worship has happened here and there in the Catholic Church and in the mainline denominations. But considerable work still needs to be done on the local church level to achieve the goals of the denominational worship renewalists.

This session introduces the heart of the liturgical renewal both in the Catholic Church and in the mainline Protestant circles.

WORSHIP RENEWAL IN THE ROMAN CATHOLIC CHURCH

The renewal of worship in the Roman Catholic Church is a complicated study that encompasses more than one hundred years and scores of promulgations and liturgical texts. In this session we will concentrate on the major document of Catholic reform, the *Constitution on the Sacred Liturgy*.

The *Constitution* views worship as the central activity of the church. Christ's work of redemption is made real through the celebration of the liturgy. What is meant by this is that worship is primarily an action from above and secondarily a response from below. When the church worships, God becomes present to give to the church the salvation that comes from Jesus Christ. As the church responds in faith, it is built into the holy temple of the Lord.

Catholic worship is defended through theological principles set forth in a section of the *Constitution*, "Nature of the Liturgy and Its Importance in the Church's Life." We may summarize these principles as follows:

- God sent his Son Jesus Christ to bring salvation to the world. "The perfect achievement of our reconciliation came forth and the fullness of divine worship was given to us."
- On the day of Pentecost, the church was called into being. The church continues in its worship to celebrate the death and resurrection of Christ and his triumph over evil.
- People are baptized into his death and resurrection; the Word proclaims his death and resurrection; the Eucharist celebrates his death and resurrection.
- The risen Christ continues to be present in his church so that all the liturgical actions of the church are Christ's actions. It is Christ who baptizes, Christ who preaches, Christ who celebrates the Eucharist.
- Through the earthly liturgy we take part in the heavenly liturgy. We join the angels, the archangels, and the heavenly host in praise of God.

- Before people are able to worship they must be called to faith and to conversion. Therefore, the liturgy proclaims the good news of salvation to those who do not believe and calls believers to continual repentance and obedience. Liturgy is the summit toward which the activity of the church is directed; at the same time it is the fount from which all the church's power flows.
- In order that the liturgy may possess its full effectiveness, it is necessary that the faithful come to it with proper dispositions, that their minds be attuned to their voices, and that they cooperate with divine grace, lest they receive it in vain.

These basic guidelines to worship underscore the gospel nature of worship reform in the Catholic Church. (The full text of the document they summarize can be found in *Twenty Centuries of Christian Worship*, pp. 317–32.) Worship proclaims, enacts, and celebrates the living, the dying, and the rising of Jesus Christ, as well as his victory over sin, death, and the powers of evil.

Worship Renewal in Mainline Protestant Churches

The reform of worship in the Roman Catholic Church soon affected the mainline churches of the Protestant world.

Unlike the Roman Catholic Church, the various Protestant churches are unable to present a united front to the world, and no document such as the *Constitution on the Sacred Liturgy* has been produced by Protestants.

A Protestant leader in worship renewal, Methodist minister, teacher, and scholar James White, described the effect of the Catholic reforms on Protestants in an essay entitled, "A Protestant Worship Manifesto," which appeared in *The Christian Century* (January 27, 1982), pp. 82–86.

He sets forth twelve reforms advocated by those working toward worship renewal:

1. Worship represents the church's unique contribution to the struggle for justice and should be shaped to reflect that understanding.

The weekly reiteration of Christ's death and resurrection should shape the attitudes and values of people in such a way that their behavior results in an obedience to God expressed in acts of justice.

2. The paschal nature of Christian worship should resound throughout all services.

Worship is grounded in God's work for us in Jesus Christ. In all worship we should experience anew the events of salvation in our own lives.

3. The centrality of the Bible in Protestant worship must be recovered. Scripture functions in the worship of many Protestant churches only as a means of reinforcing what the preacher wants to say. This makes the Bible an option rather than the source of Christian worship.

4. The importance of time as a major structure in Christian worship must be discovered.

Because the church and its worship is rooted in the saving events of Christ, the church needs to rediscover the events of salvation and mark time by the celebration of these events—Advent, Christmas, Epiphany, Lent, Holy Week, Easter, Pentecost.

5. All reforms in worship must be shaped ecumenically.

Much that is happening in worship renewal is a result of all churches borrowing from all other churches. Every church, from Orthodox to Quaker, brings something to the discussion of worship. Our worship will be enriched as we listen to each other and draw from each other's resources.

6. Drastic changes are needed in the process of Christian initiation.

Initiation into the church must be seen as a process of evangelization. There is a need to rethink how worship contributes to this.

7. High on the list of reforms is the need to recover the Eucharist as the chief Sunday service.

The prayer of thanksgiving must be rediscovered as a proclamation of the gospel. People need to be physically engaged—walking forward, standing or kneeling to receive the bread and wine, as opposed to sitting in the pew.

8. Recovering the sense of God's action in other "commonly called sacraments" is essential.

The church needs to institute additional services, such as services of reconciliation or services of healing, in which God's saving and healing presence is experienced.

9. Music must be seen in its pastoral context as fundamentally an enabler of fuller congregational participation.

Music must serve the text of worship, rather than functioning as an interruption or an interlude. Recovery of psalm singing in worship is an encouraging sign.

10. The space and furnishings for worship need substantial change in most churches.

If the quality of the worship celebration is to be improved, attention must be paid to the space in which the celebration takes place. People's visual, aural, and kinetic senses must be acknowledged.

11. No reform of worship will progress far until much more effort is invested in teaching seminarians and clergy to think through the functions of Christian worship.

Training in worship leadership must find its rightful place in the seminary curriculum.

12. Liturgical renewal is not only a changing of worship but also a reshaping of American Christianity, root and branch.

Worship renewal relates to and affects every part of the church's life.

CONCLUSION

In this session we have looked at the theology of worship renewal through a study of the *Constitution on the Sacred Liturgy,* and we have examined twelve effects of this renewal on the worship of the local church.

This study shows the extent of worship renewal—it touches every aspect of the church's ministry and life. Everything the church does is empowered by worship.

For the full text of the *Constitution on the Sacred Liturgy* and "A Protestant Worship Manifesto," see *Twenty Centuries of Christian Worship,* pp. 317–37.

┌─────────────────────────────────┐
│   STUDY GUIDE   │
└─────────────────────────────────┘

Read Session 10, "Do All in Decency and in Order,"
before starting the study guide.

PART I: PERSONAL STUDY

Complete the following questions individually.

1. *Life Connection*

◆ A very significant renewal in worship has occurred in the Roman Catholic Church and in mainline denominations since 1964. If you have not experienced worship renewal in one of these churches, you should by all means search out the experience. Call various churches and ask, "Do you practice a renewal worship?" When you find such a church, attend! Describe your response to worship renewal:_____

_____

_____

_____

2. *Content Questions*

◆ What changes took place in the Roman Mass following the promulgation of *The Constitution on the Sacred Liturgy* in 1964? _____

_____

_____

_____

◆ Describe the impact of *The Constitution on the Sacred Liturgy* on worship in mainline Protestant churches. _____

_____

_____

_____

- Changing the language of worship or the order of worship is not enough to count for worship renewal. What task still lies before the Catholic Church and mainline Protestant churches? _____

  _____

  _____

  _____

  _____

- What happens through the celebration of the liturgy in Catholic worship?

  _____

  _____

  _____

  _____

  _____

- Outline in your own words the summary of the renewal principles in Catholic worship. _____

  _____

  _____

  _____

  _____

- What principles of worship appeal to you? _____

  _____

  _____

  _____

  _____

- What problems do these principles raise for you? _____

  _____

  _____

  _____

  _____

  _____

• James White sets forth twelve reform goals for the mainline churches. List these goals according to the priority you would give them in the local church.

1. _____
2. _____
3. _____
4. _____
5. _____
6. _____
7. _____
8. _____
9. _____
10. _____
11. _____
12. _____

3. *Application*

• Think through the twelve suggestions for worship renewal, identifying which of the twelve have been fulfilled in the worship of your church.

_____
_____
_____
_____
_____
_____

PART II: GROUP DISCUSSION

The following questions are designed for group discussion.

1. *Life Connection*

• Begin your discussion by asking members of the group to comment on their experience of renewed worship either in a Roman Catholic or in a mainline Protestant church.

2. *Thought Questions*

- What do you think lies at the heart of a renewed worship? Write your answers on the board.

- Does your answer to the preceding question allow that a truly renewed worship can happen in a liturgical setting? Or do you think that a truly renewed worship will break away from the liturgy? As you give your reasons, write them on the board.

- In what ways do you agree with the principles of worship summarized from *The Constitution on the Sacred Liturgy?* Disagree? Put two columns on the board and write out the group's answers.

- Write on the board the twelve suggestions for worship renewal given by White. Now ask for a show of hands to determine their order of relative importance, as suggested by the members of the group.

3. *Application*

- Go through each of the twelve suggestions made by White, asking the following questions: (1) How has our church fulfilled this goal? (2) What does our church need to do to fulfill this goal?

Be Filled with the Spirit

A Study in Charismatic Worship

Ever since I knew I was called into the ministry, I have wanted more and more of the Holy Spirit.

When I was in college, a friend came to me and said, "Bob, a group of us are joining in a special meeting of prayer asking the Holy Spirit to fill us and to use us in ministry through the power of the Spirit. Would you like to come?" I went gladly, filled with expectation. But the administration of this conservative college closed down the prayer service for fear we were becoming too fanatical.

Throughout history there have been groups of people who claimed to be especially touched by the Holy Spirit and empowered to minister in the name of the Spirit. For the most part, the established church has responded negatively toward these groups.

The initial response of the established church toward the charismatic movement of this century was quite negative. However, many Catholics and Protestants have come to recognize the charismatic movement as a true moving of the Holy Spirit. Aspects of charismatic worship and ministry have penetrated nearly every circle of Christians.

In this study we will examine charismatic worship and ask how our church tradition might benefit from the insights and practice of charismatic worship.

Historical Background

The "charismatic renewal" of the late twentieth century is one of several movements in the history of the church to emphasize the power of God and the manifestation of miraculous and revelatory gifts of the Spirit, especially tongues and prophecy.

During the late 1960s and early 1970s the charismatic movement was described by observers as a prayer movement. The central purpose of the charismatic prayer meeting was considered to be worship. There was no prescribed agenda for the meeting, and anyone could contribute. Kilian McDonnell provided an eyewitness account of a charismatic prayer meeting. It started with a hymn followed by a Scripture reading. Then people meditated and prayed silently. After about five minutes someone prayed aloud, using as a basis the text that had just been read. This was followed by more silence, broken by short prayers from various members for the gift of praise, for strength, and for sensitivity to the needs of others. Someone with a guitar started singing a hymn, and the other members began to join in. A young businessman then gave a testimony of how God had enabled him to come to understand and to help a difficult coworker at his office since the previous meeting. Two others gave testimonies, and then there was silence for several minutes. An older man then asked for prayers regarding a domestic problem. He knelt in the middle of the room as the others gathered around and laid hands on him. One of them spoke in tongues for about half a minute while others quietly prayed in English. After three minutes he rose, and everyone sat down as before. A young girl read a psalm, and then there was silence. Someone suggested that they break for coffee.

The meeting resumed after twenty minutes, and the guitar player sang a hymn that he had written. Then there was extended silence until a man who had been there a few times previously suggested that the group pray for him to be baptized with the Holy Spirit. He knelt in the center and the others gathered around, placing hands on his head and shoulders. He did not speak in tongues at that time. After three or four minutes he rose, and everyone returned to his or her place. Somebody began to recite the Lord's Prayer and everybody else joined in. Then the members of the group began to tell of special prayer concerns. One man had an appointment for a job interview, another had housing problems, and another needed guidance for his life's direction. There was a pause, and then a member prophesied about God's mercy. After another silence, someone began singing in tongues, and three or four others joined in. The singing was followed by silence and the recitation of a psalm by the group. The entire meeting was about two and a half hours in length, which was "very modest by classical and neo-Pentecostal standards" (Kilian McDonnell, *Catholic Pentecostalism: Problems in Evaluation* [Dove, 1970], pp. 25–27).

PRINCIPLES OF CHARISMATIC WORSHIP

In an article entitled "The Theology of Charismatic Worship" in *Twenty Centuries of Christian Worship*, charismatic leader Gerrit Gustafson identifies five principles of charismatic worship:

1. Charismatic worship is based on the activation of the priesthood of all believers.

Understanding the church as a priesthood is certainly not unique to the charismatic movement. That was an emphasis fundamental to the Reformation. But these present-day Spirit-filled worshipers are achieving a new understanding of what it means to be a priest. Traditionally when we say that we are priests, we mean that we need no other mediator besides Christ. As true as that is and as revolutionary as that may have sounded in Martin Luther's day, it is only a partial understanding of what it means to be a priest. Priests not only draw near to God, they minister to God. Priests offer sacrifices.

For the charismatic, the Holy Spirit is the activator who takes us out of neutral and prompts the various expressions of worship. Worship can be understood as the grateful sacrifices offered by activated priests discovering their ministry to God.

2. Charismatic worship involves the whole person—spirit, soul, and body.

One implication of this "activation" is that worship involves action. Charismatic worship is demonstrative. It is something you do. It is not passive. Charismatic worship includes hearty singing, lifting of hands, bowing, clapping, dancing, and shouting.

3. Charismatics experience the real presence of Christ in worship.

Another key to understanding charismatic worship is the presence of God. It doesn't take many visits to charismatic worship services to hear about "entering into the presence of God." A charismatic understanding of God's presence distinguishes between omnipresence (God is everywhere at all times) and manifest presence (God is especially present at certain times and places).

A charismatic believes that the acts of giving thanks and singing are gateways to God's manifest presence (Ps 100:2, 4). Thus music is fundamental to encountering God in a charismatic worship service. The worship leader (no longer just a "song leader") becomes a vital part of the church. His or her ability to lead worship affects the congregation's experience of God's manifest presence. New skills are sometimes required to know how to choose songs and connect them so as to create a progression into God's presence.

4. Charismatics experience God's power in worship.

Closely related to the experience of entering God's presence with singing is the correlation between singing and experiencing God's power. Ps 22:3 forms the basis of a conviction commonly held among charismatics that God sits enthroned on the praise of the people. Our praise creates a throne from which God exercises divine power and might.

Faith for miracles, healing, and deliverance from evil spirits seems to come more easily following vigorous worship. American evangelist T. L. Osborne regularly played the popular charismatic worship tape, "All Hail King Jesus" for thirty minutes through loudspeakers before his crusades in Africa. He testified that miracles happened even before he preached because of the atmosphere of power that the worship music created. A Nigerian pastor commented on American Christianity with this comparison: "In America, you believe; in Nigeria, we worship."

5. Charismatic worship extends into life beyond the sanctuary.

Charismatic worship is more than music and singing. It is vigorously living a life of sacrifice to God and service to others. Paul defined worship as presenting ourselves as living sacrifices (Rom 12:1). The author of Hebrews commended God's people to vocal praise as well as good works (Heb 13:15–16). Acceptable worship requires both.

This larger view of worship explains why the charismatic movement is noted for active involvement in ministries to the poor, the abused, the addicted, and the brokenhearted, as well as in international missions. These ministries are in themselves acts of worship. Wholehearted worship in the Christian assembly, wherein we give gifts of praise to God, is a rehearsal for the life of worship that follows, wherein we give of ourselves to the needs of the world around us. If we are enthusiastic with the song, we most likely will be enthusiastic in our service.

CHARACTERISTICS OF CHARISMATIC WORSHIP

D. L. Alford has written that "freedom in worship, joyful singing, both vocal and physical expressions of praise, instrumental accompaniment of singing, and acceptance of a wide variety of music styles are all characteristic of [this] renewal. . . . It is not unusual to find worshipers singing, shouting, clapping hands, leaping, and even dancing before the Lord as they offer . . . sincere praise and thanksgiving." Alford observes that charismatic worship has several important characteristics, including (1) emphasis on the singing of psalms and songs from Scripture; (2) reliance on music for praise and worship in church, at conferences and festivals, in small groups, and in private; (3) use of musical instruments; (4) emphasis on congregational singing with the use of praise leaders; (5) use of dance and pageantry, both spontaneous and choreographed; (6) use of drama and pantomime; and (7) emphasis on the prophetic role of the musicians (S. M. Burgess and G. M. McGee, eds., *Dictionary of Pentecostal and Charismatic Movements* [Zondervan, 1988], pp. 693–94). Other characteristics of charismatic worship include the lifting up of

hands, linking arms, freedom for all participants to contribute (especially in prophetic gifts and acts of healing), and the use of music, art, and color as sacramental
signs. There is a fresh emphasis on meaning in worship and a recognition that
Scripture should be read with great emphasis and care, that actions should not be
perfunctory, and that words should correspond to actions.

THE INCORPORATION OF CHARISMATIC ELEMENTS
OF WORSHIP INTO LITURGICAL WORSHIP

By 1974 some liturgists began to discern an urgent need to incorporate distinctive
charismatic elements into their liturgies. Soon characteristics of charismatic worship came to be incorporated into the worship of both Catholics and Protestants.
The first charismatic Mass was conducted on Pentecost Monday in 1975 at St.
Peter's Basilica in Rome with Cardinal Leon Josef Suenens as celebrant.

CONCLUSION

In this session we have encountered both the breadth and the depth of the
charismatic movement and its infusion of free and joyous worship in the Spirit. We
have seen that this important tradition of worship is changing the face of modern
worship.

This chapter has drawn heavily from Richard Riss, "The Charismatic Renewal"
and Gerrit Gustafson, "A Charismatic Theology of Worship," in *Twenty Centuries of
Christian Worship*, pp. 121–25, 309–12.

STUDY GUIDE

Read Session 11, "Be Filled with the Spirit," before starting the study guide.

PART I: PERSONAL STUDY

Complete the questions below individually.

1. *Life Connection*

♦ Although charismatic worship is common throughout North America, there are many who have not yet witnessed a charismatic service. Do everything possible to visit a charismatic church in your area. There are many different kinds of charismatic churches ranging from independent charismatic to liturgical charismatic. Locate any type and visit. Describe your impressions: _____

_____

_____

_____

_____

_____

2. *Content Questions*

♦ What is the emphasis of a charismatic church? _____

_____

_____

_____

_____

♦ How was the charismatic movement first described? _____

_____

_____

_____

_____

◆ Summarize in your own words the order of an early charismatic worship service.

_____

_____

_____

_____

◆ List, in your own words, the five principles of charismatic worship.
   1. _____
   2. _____
   3. _____
   4. _____
   5. _____

◆ Define the charismatic understanding of priesthood. _____

_____

_____

_____

_____

◆ What physical and emotional elements of worship are experienced in charismatic worship? _____

_____

_____

_____

_____

◆ Define the phrase "manifest presence." _____

_____

_____

_____

_____

◆ How does one experience "manifest presence"? _____

_____

_____

_____

_____

◆ Why are charismatics heavily involved in ministries to the poor and needy? _____

_____

_____

_____

_____

_____

◆ Using your own words, list the seven characteristics of charismatic worship.

1. _____
2. _____
3. _____
4. _____
5. _____
6. _____
7. _____

◆ Using your own words, describe how charismatic worship is expressed in the liturgical tradition. _____

_____

_____

_____

_____

3. *Application*

◆ Thinking back through the material in this session, what elements of charismatic worship would you like to see expressed in the worship of your church? _____

_____

_____

_____

PART II: GROUP DISCUSSION

The following questions are designed for group discussion.

1. *Life Connection*

• Begin your group discussion by asking members of the group who have experience with charismatic worship to tell about their experiences and impressions.

2. *Thought Questions*

• Some members of the group may have fears about charismatic worship. Get these fears on the table by asking, "What kind of fears do you have about charismatic worship?"

• Do you think of yourself as a priest offering the ministry of worship to God?

• Would you feel free to dance or shout in worship or to express some kind of meaningful bodily movement, such as lifting up your hands? Explain why or why not.

• Have you ever experienced the "manifest presence"? Explain the emotional content of this experience.

• Have you ever experienced the power of God in worship through the anointing of oil or the laying on of hands? Explain the emotional content of this experience.

• Do you think the charismatic emphasis on the inner and emotional experience goes too far in one direction? If you answered in the affirmative, how would you balance it?

3. *Application*

• Do the following exercise to determine whether or not your church is open to the charismatic movement. On the left side of the board set forth your order of service in a column that goes from top to bottom. Designate this list as "Order." On the right side of the board write the word "Freedom." Now find places in the order of worship where free and spontaneous acts of charismatic worship could be incorporated. Write these acts in the right column adjacent to "Order." Put the two together to envision how your worship would look if it converged with charismatic worship.

LIFT UP YOUR HEART (AND HANDS)

A Study in Praise and Worship

I first came into contact with the praise and worship movement through Maranatha! Music. Chuck Fromm (the CEO) and I had struck up a telephone relationship that had gone on for nearly five years. Our talks, which occurred on a regular basis, covered the spread of worship from liturgical styles to praise and worship style.

In spite of our conversations, I had never really experienced a full-blown praise and worship service. In 1985 Maranatha! Music sponsored a worship workshop in Capistrano Beach, California, and I was invited to speak. The other speaker and worship leader was Graham Kendrick, well-known English song and hymn writer. I didn't know it, but I was in for some big surprises.

Not only was I astonished at the variety of musical instruments—synthesizers, drums, electric guitar, and piano—but I was swept off my feet by the enthusiasm and intense devotion of the worshipers. They worshiped with all their hearts, both hands lifted up and bodies swaying to the music.

In the last several decades this new style of worship has spread throughout North America and other parts of the world. The designation for this approach to worship that seems to be gaining most acceptance is "praise and worship" (P&W). This discussion seeks to explain what this style of worship is and to consider its effects on worship in the future.

WHERE DID PRAISE AND WORSHIP ORIGINATE?

P&W emerged from ideas that were prevalent in the sixties and early seventies. Many people found that traditional worship forms no longer spoke to them. On the other hand, people were seeking the immediacy of the Spirit and intimacy. Many felt that music and informality were necessary to connect with people in our post-Christian culture.

The early 1960s saw the rise of testimonial music, led by Bill Gaither. Songs such as "He Touched Me," "There's Something about That Name," "Let's Just Praise the Lord," and "Because He Lives" touched many lives and introduced people to a new genre of music. Although they began as performance songs, they soon became congregational: people sang along or at least joined in on the refrain. The late 1960s saw the rise of the Jesus movement on the West Coast (and all over the world), which emphasized singing praise choruses, some of which were written and sung right on the spot.

Since those early days in the 1960s and early 1970s, this form of music and the style of worship it has engendered have developed into a new worldwide approach to worship.

CHARACTERISTICS OF THE PRAISE AND WORSHIP MOVEMENT

While the exact origins of the Praise and Worship tradition are ambiguous, the movement itself is not difficult to describe.

First, P&W moves beyond a post-Enlightenment expression of worship. Since the eighteenth century, Western thought has been influenced by the Enlightenment's rationalistic and scientific explanations for our existence. Worship influenced by the Enlightenment is essentially cerebral, appealing to the mind and to the intellectual side of our beings. It is "left-brained." In contrast, P&W touches the affective side of the person. It is "right-brained," reaching into the feelings and emotions of the human personality. However, it is not correct to dismiss it as merely emotional worship or as worship lacking in content or biblical foundation.

Second, P&W seeks to recapture the lost element of praise found in both Old and New Testament worship. It stands in the tradition of the Talmud, saying, "Man should always utter praises, and then pray." Praise God, first and foremost, and then move on to the other elements of worship, say the proponents of P&W.

DISTINGUISHING PRAISE FROM WORSHIP

A major feature of the P&W movement is its tendency to distinguish praise from worship. Judson Cornwall, a P&W leader and author of more than half a dozen books, addresses the distinction between praise and worship in his book Let Us Worship (Bridge, 1983). Cornwall argues that the Scriptures present praise as something different from worship. He cites Psalm 95 as a good example of this distinction. In the opening verses (here quoted from the NIV), the psalmist invites praise:

Come, let us sing for joy to the Lord;
let us shout aloud to the Rock of our salvation.
Let us come before him with thanksgiving
and extol him with music and song. (vv. 1–2)

Only after praise has been offered does the psalmist invite worship:

Come, let us bow down in worship,
let us kneel before the Lord our Maker. (v. 6)

Cornwall concludes that "the order is praise first, worship second" (p. 143).

"Praise," Cornwall writes, "prepares us for worship." It is a "prelude to worship." Praise does not attempt to get something from God; it is a ministry that we offer to God. We offer praise for what God has done—for God's mighty deeds in history and God's continued providential presence in our lives.

Praise focuses on what God has done; worship, on who God is. The one extols the acts of God, the other the person and character of God. Cornwall clarifies this distinction between praise and worship. "Praise," he writes, "begins by applauding God's power, but it often brings us close enough to God that worship can respond to God's presence. While the energy of praise is toward what God does, the energy of worship is toward who God is. The first is concerned with God's performance, while the second is occupied with God's personage. The thrust of worship, therefore, is higher than the thrust of praise" (p. 146).

THE TEMPLE SEQUENCE

The order of the service, the transition from praise to worship, is patterned after the movement in the Old Testament tabernacle and temple from the outer court to the inner court and then into the holy of holies. This progression is accomplished through song. The song leader (or the worship leader, as she or he is more often called) plays a significant role in moving the congregation through the various steps that lead to worship.

The service begins with choruses of personal experience or testimony, such as "This Is the Day the Lord Has Made" or "We Bring Sacrifices of Praise into the House of the Lord." These songs center on praise, are upbeat in tempo, and relate to the personal experience of the believer. Many songs mention "I," "me," or "we." In terms of the tabernacle typology, this is the first step. The people are still outside the fence that surrounds the tabernacle. They cannot worship until they come through the gates into the tabernacle court.

This movement in song prepares us for what takes place in the second step. The mood and the content of the music shift to express the action of entering the gates and coming into the courts. Here the song leader chooses songs that express the transition from praise to worship. These are songs of thanksgiving, such as the Scripture song from Psalm 100: "I will enter his gates with thanksgiving in my heart, I will enter his courts with praise" or "Come let us worship and bow down, let us kneel before the Lord our God, our Maker."

According to Cornwall, "it is a matter of bringing them from a consciousness of what has been done in them and for them (testimony) to who did it in and for them (thanksgiving). The procession through the eastern gates into the outer court should be a joyful march, for thanks should never be expressed mournfully or negatively. While the people are singing choruses of thanksgiving, they will be thinking both of themselves and of their God, but by putting the emphasis upon the giving of thanks, the majority of the thought patterns should be on their God. Singing at this level will often be a beginning level of praise, but it will not produce worship, for the singers are not yet close enough to God's presence to express a worship response" (p. 156).

The third step, into the holy of holies, brings the believer away from himself or herself into a full conscious worship of God alone. The worshiper is not thinking about what God has done, but rather of who God is in person and in character. A quiet devotion hovers over the congregation as the people sing songs such as "Father, I Adore You," "I Love You, Lord," and "You Are Worthy." In these moments of worship "the emotional clapping will likely be replaced with devotional response of upturned faces, raised hands, tears, and even a subtle change in the timbre of voices." For when there is an "awareness that we have come into the presence of God, we step out of lightness with sobriety" (p. 157).

This step in the sequence is often described as an experience of "the manifest presence of God." This experience does not differ greatly from the liturgical experience of the presence of Christ at the Lord's Table. In this atmosphere the charismata, or gifts of God, are released. Just as men and women throughout the history of the church have experienced physical and spiritual healing while partaking of the table of Christ, so many today are tasting of special manifestations of the Holy Spirit in worship renewal as the Lord inhabits (i.e., settles down, abides in) the praises of the people (Ps 22:3).

PRAISE, WORSHIP, TEACHING, PRAYER, MINISTRY

It is common in the P&W tradition of worship to distinguish between the various acts of a typical service. The most significant distinction is the one that is made between praise and worship, as described above. Other acts in the service include the time for teaching, the time for intercessory prayer, and the time for ministry.

Because most P&W churches are informal, the various acts of the service are performed in an informal way. For example, teaching is fairly straightforward and may end with a time of brief feedback or discussion (depending on the size of the congregation).

Intercessory prayer may also be informal. The traditional pastoral prayer may be replaced by a prayer circle. After prayer many churches enter a time of ministry. People go into various rooms where those gifted with ministry for particular needs lay hands on them and pray for hurt and broken lives as from the Master's hand. What is experienced in this setting can be very meaningful, ministering in a powerful way to the people of God.

RESPONSE TO PRAISE AND WORSHIP

Some traditional churches have not responded to P&W at all, perhaps because they are not fully aware of the P&W tradition. These congregations may have heard P&W songs and may be vaguely aware of the existence of such a style of worship in nontraditional churches, but for the most part they are oblivious to P&W.

Other congregations are more aware of P&W but they are indifferent to it or actively dismiss it, arguing that it is "too superficial" or "too charismatic." A third set of traditional churches are not only aware of P&W and its relevancy to a post-Enlightenment culture but also seek to integrate this new approach to worship into the local church. (See "The Praise & Renewal Movement," in *Twenty Centuries of Christian Worship*, pp. 131–34.)

STUDY GUIDE

Read Session 12, "Lift Up Your Heart (and Hands),"
before starting the study guide.

PART I: PERSONAL STUDY

Complete the following questions individually.

1. *Life Connection*

- Praise and worship is a style of worship that has been adopted in many
  churches. Essentially it is chorus singing backed by many stringed instruments and characterized by intense emotion and the raising of hands.
  While this form of singing is always found in charismatic churches, it is
  being introduced into the worship of some mainline and evangelical
  churches. If you have never experienced this kind of worship, call around
  to various churches and ask, "Do you do Praise and Worship?" When you
  find such a church, visit it. Describe your impressions. _____

  _____

  _____

  _____

  _____

  _____

  _____

  _____

2. *Content Questions*

- What human needs does P&W worship address? _____

  _____

  _____

  _____

  _____

  _____

◆ What are the origins of P &W worship? _____
_____
_____
_____
_____
_____
_____

◆ How would you describe a post-Enlightenment worship? _____
_____
_____
_____
_____
_____
_____

◆ What does P&W seek to recapture? _____
_____
_____
_____
_____
_____

◆ How does P&W distinguish praise from worship? _____
_____
_____
_____
_____
_____

◆ What is the Old Testament basis for P&W worship? _____
_____
_____
_____
_____

- In the space below outline or draw a picture of the order of worship followed in P&W.

- What is the difference between songs of testimony and songs of thanksgiving?

  _____

  _____

  _____

  _____

  _____

- What songs are sung in the third step, the step that takes the worshiper into the holy of holies? _____

  _____

  _____

  _____

  _____

- How does the third phase, the experience of "the manifest presence of God," correspond to liturgical worship? _____

  _____

  _____

  _____

  _____

- Make a line that expresses the fivefold progression of worship in the Vineyard church.

- Describe the different ways in which a P&W church might approach preaching or prayer. _____
  _____
  _____
  _____

- In what three ways have traditional churches responded to P&W churches. _____
  _____
  _____
  _____

3. *Application*

- What aspects of P&W would you like to see brought into the worship of your church? Think about this and write down your ideas to share in the group discussion. _____
  _____
  _____
  _____

PART II: GROUP DISCUSSION

The following questions are designed for group discussion.

1. *Life Connection*

- Begin your discussion by asking group members who have experienced a P&W service to tell of their experience.

2. *Thought Questions*

- If there are members of the group who have fears about P&W worship, it may be a good idea to air them. What are their fears and where do they come from?

- Do you think the worship of your church would be characterized as pre-Enlightenment or post-Enlightenment? Explain.

- Do you experience intimacy in the worship of your church? If not, how do you think the approach of P&W would help you achieve greater intimacy in your worship?

- Do you think it is appropriate to develop a Christian worship order based on the Old Testament? Or should a Christian worship order be based on the New Testament? If so, what passage or description of worship is appropriate?

- Have you ever experienced "the manifest presence" of God in either song or Communion? If so, describe it. If not, explain why you have not experienced it.

3. *Application*

- Write the word "order" at the top of the left side of the board. Now write down the order of your worship from top to bottom. Ask, "What is the actual progression of our worship? Where does it lead us? Does it take us into manifest presence?"

- On the right side, write "P&W order." Follow the progression of this order from the entrance through the gates, through the outer court, into the inner court, and finally to the holy of holies. What songs would you sing (hymns and choruses) to express the progression of worship? Write the titles into your order.

- Is there some way you can merge your tradition of worship with the P&W tradition? Explore the possibility.

THE FUTURE OF CHRISTIAN WORSHIP

A *Study in the Convergence of Worship Traditions*

In 1988 Chuck Fromm of Maranatha! Music asked me to oversee a conference on worship to be held in Irvine, California.

Since Maranatha! Music was hosting the conference, I asked Chuck what he wanted. "You are in charge," he answered. "Do whatever you feel led to do."

Astonished at this opportunity, I said, "Well, Chuck, I'll tell you what I've been thinking a lot about lately."

"What?"

"Well, I've been wondering what a conference would be like if we brought together liturgical, free church, praise and worship and charismatic people."

Chuck's eyes grew big as he said, "Yes, I like that idea—go for it."

We did.

People came to our conference from all over the United States. For three days we listened to each other and worshiped in each other's styles. On the final day we experimented with a blended service that turned out to be a powerful experience for us all.

This final session of *Rediscovering the Missing Jewel* focuses on the convergence movement in worship—a movement that draws from various worship traditions and blends them into one.

WHAT IS CONVERGENCE WORSHIP

Randy Sly and Wayne Boosahda, ministers in blended worship churches, have written about the convergence movement (which we will abbreviate CM) in *Twenty Centuries of Christian Worship*. Here we draw upon their work. Arising out of a common desire and hunger to experience the fullness of Christian worship and spirituality, CM seeks to blend or merge the essential elements in the Christian faith, as represented by three major streams of thought and practice: the liturgical/sacramental, the evangelical/Reformed, and the charismatic. An increasing number of local congregations and leaders from many backgrounds are finding "new treasures as well as old" in the spiritual heritage of the church universal.

A Brief Historical Background of Convergence Worship

The convergence movement has clear antecedents in two major movements of spiritual and worship renewal: the charismatic movement and the liturgical renewal movement in both Catholic and mainline Protestant churches. The charismatic renewal began in the early 1960s primarily within mainline denominations. Those in the renewal saw a blending of charismatic or Pentecostal elements, such as healing, prophecy, and spontaneous worship and praise, with the more traditional elements of mainline (and eventually Roman Catholic) liturgical practices.

The other key influence on CM has been the liturgical renewal movement in nineteenth-century France and England. The liturgical renewal caused a resurgence of interest in recapturing the essence, spirit, and shape of ancient Christian worship as practiced and understood by the church of the first eight centuries. Particular emphasis was placed on the fathers of the ancient, undivided church until about 390 CE. The recovery of the theology and practice of worship and ministry during that fertile era overflowed into the mainline Protestant churches and began to have major impact on them from the 1950s onward.

A common component in the current CM, which came from these earlier movements, is a strong sense of concern for unity in the whole of Christ's body, the church. Those involved in CM seem broadly gripped by the hunger and desire to learn from traditions of worship and spirituality other than their own and to integrate these discoveries into their own practice and experience in the journey of faith.

Common Concerns of Convergence Worship

Those who are being drawn into this convergence of streams can be characterized by several common elements. While these traits are not exhaustive and are not presented in any order of importance, they explain the focus and direction of the convergence movement.

1. A restored commitment to the sacraments, especially the Lord's Table.

Some churches have seen Holy Baptism and Holy Communion more as ordinances than as sacraments. They are understood as commands from the Lord that the church must obey, for no other purpose than that of obedience.

A more sacramental view understands these two expressions of church life as a symbol used as a point of contact between people and God. The Lord's presence and power are released in these acts as the worshiper encounters God in water, bread, and wine.

2. An increased motivation to know more about the early church.

Studying the early church has given many an opportunity to see New Testament principles being applied by those who were discipled by the Twelve and by those who followed them. These writings provide a window into an earlier time, explaining how the early church approached faith and practice, how it worshiped, and how it established leadership for a growing movement. It is believed that the bloodline of the body of Christ can be traced through succeeding generations, revealing both the successes and failures in the faith.

3. A love for the whole church and a desire to see the church as one.

Convergence churches appreciate the gifts that each stream of the church provides to the whole. The call of the CM churches is to "be one," to move together in presenting a people united under Christ to reach a hurting world.

4. The blending in the practice of all three streams is evident, yet each church approaches convergence from a unique point of view.

A church does not necessarily have to change its identity when it becomes a part of a convergence movement. Most convergence churches have a dominant base, one particular expression of the church that regulates the others. They can still look very Episcopalian, Orthodox, Baptist, Nazarene, independent charismatic, and so on, while including additional elements of worship and ministry from other streams.

5. An interest in integrating structure with spontaneity in worship.

Liturgies are being reintroduced into the church to bring a balance in worship among all the elements that Scripture has revealed as necessary for worshiping God in spirit and in truth. As noted earlier, the word "liturgy" literally means the "work of the people." Through the introduction of liturgical elements, worship becomes the work of the body in praise, repentance, the hearing of the Word, and the celebration of Christ's death and resurrection. Within these forms room can always be found for the spontaneous moving of the Spirit.

The historic creeds of the church, especially the Apostle's Creed and the Nicene Creed, are once again giving the body of Christ the foundational roots of orthodoxy. The *Book of Common Prayer* and other liturgical resources are also being blended with spontaneous praise and worship in convergence churches. The Lord's Supper is being celebrated with a greater understanding of the sacredness of the event, and churches are following the Christian year and liturgical calendar more consistently as a means of taking congregations on an annual journey of faith. All of these expressions give local fellowships a greater sense of connection with the church worldwide and with the church through history.

6. A greater involvement of sign and symbol in worship.

The contemporary church has begun to reclaim the arts for Christ. Signs and symbols point beyond themselves to a greater truth and serve as contact points for apprehending inward spiritual reality. Banners and pageantry have found a new place in the church. Crosses and candles now adorn processionals in some churches that, for years, had looked on pageantry as the death knell of a vital faith. Crosses and Christian art are appearing in contexts where they had been absent before.

7. A continuing commitment to personal salvation, biblical teaching, and the work and ministry of the Holy Spirit.

The convergence movement is definitely not the abandonment of a stream but a convergence of streams. The work of God is inclusive, not exclusive, bringing forth from each tributary those things that God has authenticated. Such issues as evangelism, missions, and the work of ministry by the power of the Spirit remain intact in this journey. The Spirit's power continues to be released in marvelous ways in people's lives, bringing about conversion, healing, release from bondages, and change in the direction of life.

Future Trends

It appears that the future of the church will be greatly affected by the convergence movement. Walls between groups and denominations are already becoming veils that can be torn down, giving those from the different branches of the church greater opportunity to experience one another's faith and practice.

The material in this session is based on Randy Sly and Wayne Boosahda, "The Convergence Movement," in *Twenty Centuries of Christian Worship*, pp. 134–40.

Read Session 13, "The Future of Christian Worship,"
before starting the study guide.

PART I PERSONAL STUDY

Complete the following questions individually .

1. *Life Connection*

◆ Although more and more churches are converging traditional and contemporary worship, there are not enough of these churches to be able to
find one in every town or village or even city. Nevertheless, an experience of convergence worship would help you understand this lesson
more clearly. The closest you can come to this may be a liturgical church
that incorporates P&W or charismatic elements. Call around and find
such a church to attend. Then write out your impression of it. _____

_____

_____

_____

_____

2. *Content Questions*

◆ How would you define convergence worship? _____

_____

_____

_____

_____

◆ What are the three streams of thought from which the convergence
movement draws? _____

_____

_____

_____

◆ What are the two antecedents of the convergence movement? _____

_____

_____

_____

_____

◆ What does the charismatic movement bring to convergence movement?

_____

_____

_____

_____

◆ What does the liturgical movement bring to the convergence movement?

_____

_____

_____

_____

◆ What is the attitude of convergence churches toward the universal body
of Christ? _____

_____

_____

_____

◆ In your own words, list the seven common concerns of convergence worship.
1. _____
2. _____
3. _____
4. _____
5. _____
6. _____
7. _____

◆ How does CM view the sacraments? _____

_____

_____

_____

_____

◆ Why is CM interested in the early church? _____

_____

_____

_____

_____

◆ What kind of church unity does CM espouse?_____

_____

_____

_____

_____

◆ How does convergence change the character of the church? _____

_____

_____

_____

_____

_____

◆ How does CM approach the liturgies of the ancient church? _____

_____

_____

_____

_____

_____

◆ How does CM view sign and symbol? _____

_____

_____

_____

_____

◆ How does CM describe its commitment to traditional matters of faith such as personal salvation, biblical teaching, and the ministry of the Holy Spirit?

_____

_____

_____

_____

_____

◆ What can CM do for the church? _____

_____

_____

_____

_____

_____

PART II: GROUP DISCUSSION

The following questions are designed for group discussion.

1. *Life Connection*
◆ Begin your discussion by asking members of the group to comment on their experience of convergence worship. If no one has experienced convergence worship, ask people to use their imaginations to describe what it might look like and what its substance and emotional content might be.

2. *Thought Questions*
◆ What kind of fears do you experience when you think about the conver- gence movement of worship?

- What kinds of hopes do you experience when you think about convergence worship?

- Would this church agree or disagree with the attitude of CM toward the sacraments? Put your arguments on the board.

- Would this church agree or disagree with the CM attitude toward the early church? Put your arguments on the board.

- Would this church agree or disagree with the CM attitude toward the unity of the church? Put your arguments on the board.

- How would convergence worship change the character of your church?

- Would your church be willing to draw worship resources from the early church?

- What could CM do for this church? Put your answers on the board.

3. *Application*

- On the left side of the chalkboard write the word "order." Under that word put the order of your worship, starting at the top and moving to the bottom. On the right side of the board write the word "convergence." Under that word place the elements of worship, drawn from both liturgical sources and praise and worship sources, that could enrich your worship.

- What would you have to do to effect convergence worship in your church?